Short-h

Sailing

L

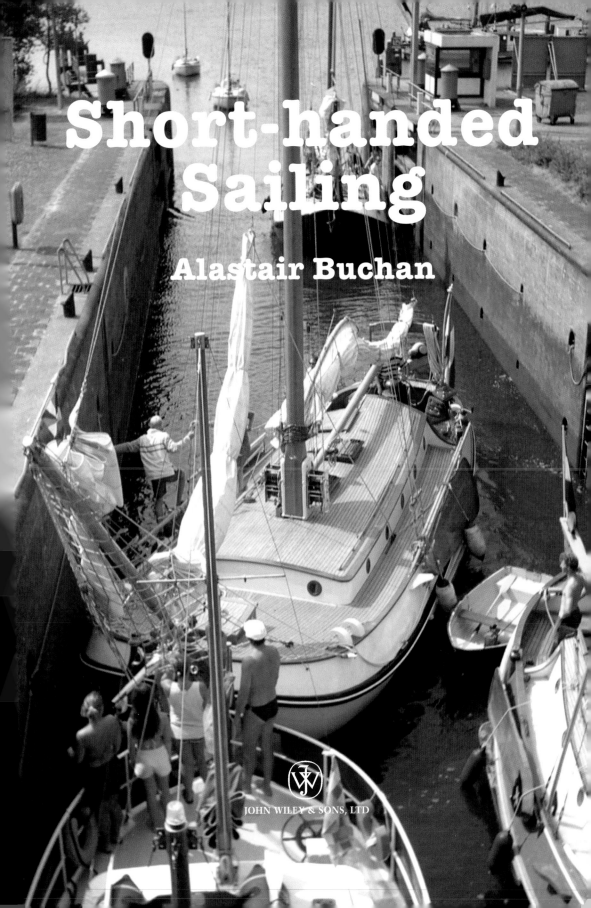

Short-handed Sailing

Alastair Buchan

JOHN WILEY & SONS, LTD

Published under the Fernhurst imprint by John Wiley & Sons Ltd , The Atrium, Southern Gate, Chichester, West Sussex PO19 8SQ, England

Telephone (+44) 1243 779777

Email (for orders and customer service enquiries): cs-books@wiley.co.uk
Visit our Home Page on www.wiley.com

Other Wiley Editorial Offices

John Wiley & Sons Inc., 111 River Street, Hoboken, NJ 07030, USA

Jossey-Bass, 989 Market Street, San Francisco, CA 94103-1741, USA

Wiley-VCH Verlag GmbH, Boschstr. 12, D-69469 Weinheim, Germany

John Wiley & Sons Australia Ltd, 42 McDougall Street, Milton, Queensland 4064, Australia

John Wiley & Sons (Asia) Pte Ltd, 2 Clementi Loop #02-01, Jin Xing Distripark, Singapore 129809

John Wiley & Sons Canada Ltd, 22 Worcester Road, Etobicoke, Ontario, Canada M9W 1L1

Wiley also publishes its books in a variety of electronic formats. Some content that appears in print may not be available in electronic books.

British Library Cataloguing in Publication Data
A catalogue record for this book is available from the British Library

ISBN-10 1-904475-21-3
ISBN-13 978-1-904475-21-7

Designed and typeset by Creative Byte
Printed in China through World Print
This book is printed on acid-free paper responsibly manufactured from sustainable forestry in which at least two trees are planted for each one used for paper production.

Cover image courtesy Sweden Yachts AB.

Contents

1 Introduction

I never set out to sail alone. It just happened. For years I wandered the coasts of Britain and Europe in a Hurley 20 called Mintaka. Like many, when I could not find a crew, I took to sailing single-handed. Initially my solo passages were modest, hardly more than a long day sail, but you can circumnavigate Britain in daily hops and one summer I did. Gradually I began modifying Mintaka to make life easier. First came a second-hand Navik self-steering gear, then head and mainsail reefing systems. I played around with leading halyards aft to the cockpit for several years till I found an arrangement that worked, and the accommodation was tweaked until life below was reasonably civilised in harbour and at sea. I was learning the tricks of short-handed sailing the hard way.

The history of short-handed sailing goes back to the late 19th century when it seemed as if flotillas of small yachts, many single-handed, were crossing the Atlantic. Howard Blackburn crossed the Atlantic single-handed twice and gave new twist to single-handed sailing, as years before he set out he had lost the fingers on both hands. Joshua Slocum circumnavigated the world in Spray and made single-handed sailing sound easy and fun. Captain John Voss disapproved of Slocum's enthusiasm for single-handed sailing and set out to show how it should be done with a crew in a converted dugout canoe, bought from Canadian Indians, and called Tillikum. Captain Voss believed in sea anchors and you get the impression that whenever he met a gale he threw out his sea anchor and the seas calmed. When his crew fell overboard and drowned he discovered that he was perfectly happy sailing alone.

Around the same time and nearer home, yachtsmen like EF Knight and Erskine Childers began the tradition of short-handed cruising around European coasts that persists to this day. In the 1950s a revival of bluewater sailing saw many of the early pioneers' feats repeated. This culminated in 1960 with the first single-handed trans-Atlantic race, where the handful of boats taking part lit the fuse to an explosion in long distance short- and single-handed sailing and the development of equipment to ease a short-handed sailor's workload.

Compared to the pioneers we have it easy. They had no self-steering and their sail handling systems were designed by pharaohs to keep slaves busy. Sails were of canvas and ropes were of hemp, manila and sisal. These are all hard to handle when wet and will rot before your eyes if given the chance. Not surprisingly, tales of their voyages are peppered with accounts of bad weather and battles with recalcitrant sails that, given half a chance, would flog themselves to tatters.

Although over a third of UK yachtsmen sometimes sail solo, and even more short-handed, somehow short- and single-handed sailing is regarded as a minority activity. The image of the lone sailor is of a nautical hermit wandering the oceans and actively rejecting the company of others. Blue water solo sailors are frequently asked, 'How do you manage by yourself?' meaning not, 'How do you sail the boat?' but 'How do you survive the solitude?' Since most people have never been truly alone they see isolation as a problem, perhaps even a danger, to be overcome. I am not sure this is true but like most single-handed sailors, far from knowing the answer I have not even considered the question and retreat behind inane remarks like, 'There's always plenty to do'.

Short-handed sailing is a broad church with room for all persuasions. For every blue water solo sailor there are a hundred who mix and match, sailing with family or friends one weekend and by themselves the next. There are those who day sail happily by themselves but would never consider an overnight passage alone and those who cheerfully cruise for weeks by themselves provided that family and friends

SOME TRANSATLANTIC CROSSINGS BY SAILING CRAFT

VESSEL	LOA(Ft)	FROM	TO	YEAR
Nonpareil	25	New York	Southampton	1868
Centennial	20	Gloucester Mass	Abercastle Wales	1876
New Bedford	19.6	Chatham Mass	Newlyn Cornwall	1877
Nautilus	19	Beverley Mass	Mullion Cornwall	1878
Little Western	16	Gloucester Mass	Cowes IOW	1880
Little Western	16	London	Halifax NS	1881
City of Bath	18	Newfoundland	Falmouth Cornwall	1881
City of Ragusa	20	Cork	Boston Mass	1887
Sea Serpent	15	Boston Mass	Coverack Cornwall	1891
Sapolio	14.5	Atlantic City	Fuzetta Portugal	1892
Richard K Fox	18	New York	Scilly Isles	1897
Great Republic	25	Gloucester Mass	Lisbon Portugal	1901
Columbia II	19	Halifax Nova Scotia	Gibraltar	1903
Vraad	18	Shetland	St John's NF	1904
Captaine Cook	18	France	Cape Cod	1905
Inga	21.25	Lisbon	La Guaira Venz	1905
Lamerhak II	23	Las Palmas	Puerto Rico	1905
Monsunen	23	La Coruña	Miami	1905
Deben Peace	24	Casablanca	WI	1905
Wanda	24	Bermuda	Eng;and	1905
Jason	25	Canary Islands	W Indies	1905
Deutscher Sport	21.5	Lisbon	St Thomas WI	1928
Dal	24	Plymouth	New York	1933
Trade Wind	25	Lisbon	New York	1933
Adventure	22	Miami	Falmouth	1947
Nova Espero	20.5	Dartmouth NS	Dartmouth England	1949
Oregon	25	La Coruña	Carslisle Bay Barbados	1950
Sopranio	19.7	Casablanca	Bridgetown Barbados	1951
Nova Espero	20	Dartmouth	Shelburne NS	1951
L'Heritique	15	Casablanca	Bridgetown	1952
Felicity Ann	23	Casablanca	P'mouth Dominica	1952
Wanderer II	24	Gibraltar	Panama	1952
Hippocapme	18	Toulon	New York	1955
Skaffie	20	Maderia	Barbados	1955
Liberia II	23.5	Las Palmas	St Croix VI	1955
L'Egare	17	Halifax NS	Falmouth	1956
Liberia III	17	Las Palmas	St Martin	1956
Tangora	23.5	Las Palmas	Trinadad	1956
Buttercup	25	Las Palmas	Babados	1956
Tethys	25	Tangier	New York	1959
Cape Horn	21.25	Plymouth	New York	1960
Eira	25	Plymouth	New York	1960
Isis	25	La Croisic	New York	1960
English Rose III	20	Cape Cod	Inishmore	1966
Super Silver	20	St John's NF	Blacksod Bay	1969
Corrie Bee	20	Plymouth	English Harbour	1978
Yankee Girl	10	Norfolk Virgina	Falmouth	1979

join them from time to time to hear of their exploits.To claim one form of short-handed sailing is better or more demanding than another is silly. Every short-hander sailor faces the same problems of passage planning and boat handling. Every solo skipper walks the high wire balancing competing demands on his time. A solo overnight coastal passage may not carry the cachet of an ocean crossing but the worries of weather, pinpoint navigation, busy shipping lanes, pot buoys and objective dangers make it as challenging and often more dangerous. The sight of land, however distant, terrifies most blue water sailors. Bill King, solo circumnavigator, considered coastal sailing so hazardous that when he was in coastal waters he took a crew whenever possible.

The difference between solo coastal and ocean passages is mostly of scale. Unlike the coastal cruiser whose exposure to the pressures of being alone lasts only hours and whose problems are solved quickly or not all, the solitary blue water cruiser measures his stress in weeks but his problems become old, familiar friends, whose idiosyncrasies are tolerated and are dealt with at a gentler pace. It is the difference between a sprinter and a marathon runner.

Somebody, somewhere, has almost certainly prepared a personality profile of the single-handed sailor. It would make interesting reading, but ticking boxes will not be of much value to the would-be single-hander who wants to know if solo sailing is for him. I know no shorebound answer to that question. Being a social isolate is not essential. If single-handed sailors are loners, then they are the most sociable loners in the world. Their cruises tend to be one long party interrupted by the occasional sail to a different location. It is a busy social life.

My first port of call in Les Saintes was the Anse du Bourg on Terre de Haut but I found the anchorage crowded and uncomfortable and the streets ashore full of noisy mopeds so I headed for what looked from the chart for a quiet anchorage in Anse Sous Vent on the uninhabited Islet A'Cabrit, a couple of miles away, only to discover friends that I had not seen for months had exactly the same idea. My anchor had barely reached the sandy bottom before the first invitation for drinks arrived and when I took that up I was ordered to that evening's beach BBQ.

Nor is sailing alone a path leading to deeper truths or the meaning of life. Reading this book, or any other, will not tell you if you can sail solo. I suspect the only sure way of finding an answer is to sail on your own. If you enjoy it then it is for you. If not, then put that voyage down to experience and look for a crew.

At least you will know for certain that single-handed sailing is not for you and plan accordingly. But just because you chose sail with a crew do not assume that you are not short-handed. Short voyages and kind weather can conceal the truth that many yachtsmen, who would never consider leaving the pontoon without company and would vehemently deny ever considering sailing solo are a whisker from unwittingly joining the ranks of those who sail alone. Regardless of how many people are aboard, if the skipper is the only person competent to stand a watch then he is effectively sailing single-handed. He must either be in the cockpit or on call for the duration of the voyage. He makes every decision, however minor, and then oversees its execution. This describes the single-handed sailor's life afloat.

Skippers with inexperienced or incompetent crews who require constant instruction and

supervision have a hard time. Nothing can be taken for granted. Lack of initiative amongst crew is as much a blessing as a curse, for unwanted enterprise is dangerous. The skipper issues instructions for even the smallest task and can never rely on it being executed properly never mind promptly. From the moment he casts off until he berths the responsibility for the safety and well-being of the crew niggles at him like toothache.

In the early part of a voyage or with the arrival of bad weather the skipper of such crews may find himself alone in the cockpit while his crew lie below, prostrate with seasickness. Some incapacitated crew members, clutching to the erroneous belief that looking towards the horizon is a sure cure for seasickness, huddle be-hooded and useless in the cockpit. They insist fresh air is good, defiantly rejecting suggestions to go below. They puke over the compass and court hypothermia until they become comatose and are carried to a bunk. If there is an emergency then lord help the skipper. At least the single-handed sailor has only his own incompetence and temporary lack of sea legs to worry him.

Mum and Dad sailing with the kids is a special case. Often only one parent is competent to take command and if that parent is out of action the other is confronted with what politicians call 'hard choices'. Even if both parents are able sailors, in an emergency one will be tasked to look after the children to the exclusion of all else. The other is left to sort the problem out and faces exactly the same challenges as a single-handed sailor but without the benefit of having thought through the options beforehand. This is hindsight speaking. When my kids were young I never realised how close to the wind I was sailing.

Many years ago we were creeping into an anchorage. Liz was on the helm. I stood in the bows and our new firstborn was asleep below. At just the right moment I cried, 'Way enough' There was an answering cry of 'The Baby!' from the cockpit and when I looked round I discovered that I was alone on deck, the helm was abandoned and the beach was fast approaching. As I rushed back to the cockpit a couple of small boys building sand castles advised me that the water was getting shallow. Now I see it as part of a learning curve. Then it was good grounds for divorce.

It is more than a question of numbers aboard and their ability. When couples sail together the person on watch is sailing single-handed for the duration of their watch, and the boat is being sailed single-handed 24 hours a day. If there is a task requiring two people, such as reefing, then the person off watch is dragged out of bed to help and, as a result, neither ever receives enough proper rest.

Anyone who believes they always sail with a full crew will have a boat set up to keep the crew busy. A walk round any boat show reveals that many production yachts have cockpits planned around the principle of providing work for willing crews of thousands. Sometimes the cockpit layout makes it difficult, even impossible, for the helmsman to steer and reach the sheets at the same time. Evolutions, even one as simple as tacking, becomes at least a two-man task with one person on the helm and another on the sheets. Reefing the mainsail takes a minimum of three people, and changing sails a small army.

Normally this is unimportant, but if for some reason you unexpectedly find yourself sailing single-handed it can create so many unforeseen problems that the boat is almost unmanageable.

On every boat the cockpit is always large enough to take the entire crew at one sitting. This makes them unnaturally large on small boats. The only reason I can see for this is that designers assume everyone aboard sits in the cockpit holding hands for the entire passage, every passage, and as a corollary, no one ever goes below at sea. This would explain why on so many boats the quality of life below decks at sea barely reaches that of a slum clearance project. I have never under-stood why being tired, cold, wet and living in squalor is supposed to be both enjoyable and character building.

The occasional single- or short-handed sailor may baulk at the effort and expense of

modifying his boat for short-handed sailing. Windvane self-steering systems, and in-mast or in-boom mainsail reefing systems are not cheap. There is nothing wrong with sailing your boat as it is or with minimal modifications but you must factor the effects of your decision into your planning, for there is more to short-handed sailing than setting up the boat to minimise the lack of numbers.

Short-handed sailing is a different mindset. Compared to the skipper of a fully crewed boat the short-handed sailor takes a very different approach to passage planning, passage making, and crew organisation. Just carrying out evolutions short-handed must be pre-planned, and probably require modifications to your boat. Short-handed skippering is not an option or fall back position that you can pull out of the hat when problems arise on passage. It is a skill that needs to be learnt and every passage requires careful planning and preparation before you even think about casting off.

The purpose of this book is to show you how to go about becoming a short-handed sailor. This is not the same as claiming to have all the answers. No one and certainly no book can ask all the questions, far less provide all the answers. It attempts to describe short-handed techniques, and the thinking behind them. Nothing is carved in stone. There are no formulaic routines that, slavishly followed, promise success every time. Even simple, repetitive events such as berthing or tacking are slightly different on every occasion. The principles remain constant but how you follow them varies to suit your circumstances.

These circumstances include you. We all bring a unique baggage of preferences, experience and expertise to every task. What works for one person will be a disaster for another. Hopefully this book will help you find the solutions that suit you and your style of sailing. Throughout, let the principle of the 'Seven Ps' dominate your thinking. It was taught to me many years ago in a different world. It is, 'proper planning and preparation prevents pretty poor performance.' This is the expurgated version. Take your pick. Both versions hold true.

2   The Boat

All boats are a compromise. If you are looking for a safe, solid cruiser that wins races, sleeps six in separate cabins each with en suite heads, and needs no more than a lick and a promise between seasons, dream on. Adding 'suitable for single or short-handed cruising' to your wish list turns dreams into nightmares. Boat builders see no market here, although some may make a token gesture by bringing every halyard aft to the cockpit.

CHOICE OF BOAT
Almost any boat can be sailed single- or short-handed. Some are better suited than others and some require above average effort to sail but there is no single ideal boat or ideal type of boat for short-handed sailing.

There are very few opportunities for the average yachtsman to take part in single- or short-handed racing. Almost without exception these are high-profile events and participation needs a very high level of personal commitment and extraordinarily generous sponsorship. The organisers will impose their requirements on the type of vessel, how it is equipped and how

experienced you must be before allowing you to participate. This is beyond the scope of this book.

Cruising is where most single-handed sailors are found. You may choose between:
* coastal cruising;
* offshore cruising;
* blue water cruising;
* trailer sailing;
* open boat sailing.

These activities are not mutually exclusive. Boats fitted out for one form of short-handed cruising can, all else equal and if you want, take part in any sort of short-handed passage. I would not sail an open boat or an inflatable across the Atlantic but it has been done, several times.

TYPE OF BOAT
The boat that suits you best balances your type of sailing against your bank balance. There is no perfect boat. Go to Las Palmas on Gran Canaria any year around the beginning of November and you will find the marina and anchorage crowded with

Gaff Sail: Traditional Dutch dinghy with leeboards.

Gaffer: originally a fishing boat and now restored.

Gaffer 2: another restored gaffer under full sail in Bequia where it earns its keep on charter.

Ketch with boomed jib for ease of sail handling.

Junk Rig, Barbados: this 20-foot junk rigged yacht successfully crossed the Atlantic.

boats preparing to sail to the Caribbean. Most are short-handed, some are fully crewed and a few single-handed. No two boats are alike, and without exception, their crews will swear with their last breath that they have the ideal short-handed boat.

So do not overlook your existing boat. It has a lot going for it. You know it, warts and all, and have probably made many of the modifications needed for short-handed sailing. If you are starting from scratch and buying a new or second-hand boat, then identify your principal sailing interest and buy a boat suited to that activity.

Some hull forms provide greater internal accommodation than others. This is usually at the expense of performance. Boats can be buxom and boxy or sleek and fast but, rarely, buxom and fast.

Lanteen Rig: only ever seen these in Las Palmas in the Canary Islands where they are raced with a crew of thousands. Tacking is a team effort to swing the yard round the mast.

Light displacement yachts are fast and place a premium on windward performance but are unforgiving of errors either in the way they are set up or how they are sailed. These boats are popular and put up truly astounding performances, but they are demanding to sail and place considerable strain on their crews. The standard of accommodation rarely rises above that found in a one-man mountain tent. Heavy displacement yachts are more stable, much slower, less demanding to sail and much more forgiving of errors. They will sail themselves for long periods but are slower to respond when carrying out manoeuvres, and once a manoeuvre is started they react badly or not all to sudden changes of mind. In light winds their performance is poor to non-existent but they are more comfortable to live aboard than a light displacement boats

Aft cockpits can feel exposed in big following seas especially in light displacement yachts with an open stern. Centre cockpit yachts normally have fairly deep cockpits and provide a feeling of absolute security but they require long control lines for self-steering. In both aft and centre cockpits protection from weather and seas comes in the form of a pramhood or a doghouse.

Extreme angles of heel make life uncomfortable. Crashing to windward through the waves is a pretty picture for others to admire but when you are on passage for several days (or weeks), once the angle of heel exceeds 20^0 even the simplest task becomes a chore and movement around the boat tiring. On monohulls the only solution is to reef and bring the boat upright.

Phil Bolger Design: Phil is renowned for his unusual designs. This is a cat-rigged, shallow-draft yacht with its centreboard offset to starboard. Note the absence of a pointed bow. This is deliberate.

Sloop, Las Palmas.

On multihulls it is best to panic when they sail at high angles of heel. They also slam and thump a seaway. When running in strong winds they can begin to surf and risk broaching or pitch poling. Cruising multihulls reduce this danger by fitting shorter masts compared to a similar sized monohull. Even so they often require someone on the helm, which imposes considerable strain on short-handed crews. The Swales helmed for much of their circum-navigation in their catamaran *Anneliese*. Multihulls are also very sensitive to their all-up weight and if their recommended maximum is exceeded, performance suffers. Forget speed, on most cruising multihulls passage times are on a par with similar sized monohulls.

If you buy a new (to you) boat you must add the costs of the modifications to the purchase price. Two obvious areas are sail handling and self-steering. Less obvious are improving liveability and safety above and below decks. At the planning stage it is easy to underestimate the amount and complexity of the work, and as a consequence your estimates are unduly optimistic.

On paper, building from scratch, finishing a kit boat, or completing a partially finished home-built boat is cheaper than buying a new factory produced boat but the savings you see are often a mirage. When you buy fixtures and fittings wholesalers' and chandlers' mark-ups are unavoidable. You pay more, sometimes several times more, than the professional boat builder. Using cheap, second-rate materials and tools is false economy. Good second-hand timber can be found in scrapyards but only if you know your wood. Occasionally genuine bargains can be picked up but when you are costing the work, use figures based on the going rate.

Without a suitable back garden you must rent yard space. This may cost close to keeping your boat afloat in a marina. Weather protection is essential and the price of buying or hiring decent scaffold tenting hurts your wallet. Cheap and cheerful lightweight polythene sheeting or tarpaulins will not survive the first strong wind. Inevitably the work will take far longer than you first thought and costs will increase. A good rule of thumb is to double or even treble your estimate of the time you need for the work and multiply the costs by four. It lessens the shock.

I write from bruising experience. I once tried my hand at building a yacht from scratch. I cut

Traditional yachts.

This home-built sloop sailed to Las Palmas from Sweden and the successfully crossed the Atlantic.

costs by using the garage, with a temporary extension, as a yard and the dining room as a store. My family were remarkably tolerant when the stench of styrene filled the house. I learned a lot about yachts and their construction but mostly it taught me that anyone taking this route to getting afloat must enjoy yacht building as much as sailing.

Annual running costs are in direct proportion to boat size. The smaller the boat the less you pay in marina charges and the annual refit requires less paint and varnish. Sails are cheaper to replace. Blocks, winches, halyards and rigging are all lighter, smaller and cheaper to renew. It pays to check these costs out before buying a boat or you may find yourself working hard to pay for keeping the boat on a pontoon.

ACCOMMODATION

Yachts between 18-25 feet normally come with two berths in the forepeak and two or three in the main cabin. Usually between the forepeak and main cabin are the heads to port and a hanging locker to starboard. The galley, which is only used in harbour, doubles as the chart table, and stowage is provided either in the form of open trough lockers or under the bunks, which are also seats except when they are beds. This is fine for living out of a seabag over a weekend provided everyone goes to bed at the same time. It is just about acceptable for a short cruise but for extended cruising the maximum that can live aboard is two.

ANNUAL RUNNING COSTS CHECKLIST

Note: This does not include the costs of buying large items of equipment or a major refit.

Serial	HEADING	AMOUNT	REMARKS
	MARINA		
1	Annual Berthing Charges		
2	Lift out		
3	Lift in		
4	Pressure Wash		
5	Un-stepping mast		
6	Stepping mast		
7	Cradle Hire		
8	Mast Storage		
9	Car Parking		
	Sub Total		
	TRAVEL		
10	Travel between home and Marina		
	Sub Total		
	MAINTENANCE		
11	Engine Maintenance		
12	Sail Valeting		
13	Anti-fouling		
14	Paints and Varnishes		
15	Rigging and lines		
16	Hull cleaner		
17	Hull polish		
18	Cloths		
19	Protective clothing & equipment		
20	Contingencies		
	Sub Total		
	ADMINISTRATION		
21	Insurance		
22	Ship's Radio Licence		
23	Harbour Dues/ Licence		
	Sub Total		
	ANNUAL CRUISING		
24	Overnight Marina Charges		
25	Fuel		
26	Charts		
27	Pilots		
28	Almanac/Tide Tables		
	Sub Total		
	GRAND TOTAL		

Another home-built 20-foot sloop. This time in steel, which not only went on to cross the Atlantic but continue across the Caribbean and on to India.

Boomed Jib and Jib: an unusual arrangement of twin jibs, both boomed. Ideal for downwind sailing, especially in the Trades.

Even then it is only possible to separate social and sleeping facilities in harbour when the forepeak becomes a bedroom and the main cabin general living space. On passage the settees in the main cabin double up as bunks. It is not until around 40 feet LOA that that there is a proper separation between living and sleeping accommodation at sea.

SIZE OF BOAT

Small boats are more easily handled than larger boats; gear is lighter and everything requires less effort. As boats increase in size mechanical or hydraulic assistance is used to reduce effort but what if the gadgetry fails? Can you raise the anchor single-handed by muscle power if your power winch fails? Can you rig some alternative to muscle power?

Regardless of aids and devices to take the strain, at some point, probably around 60 feet, a yacht will become too large for the average single or short-handed crew to handle safely. Bigger does not always mean quicker. In 1972 Jean-Yves Terlain entered Vendredi Treize (128 ft/39m) in the single-handed Trans-Atlantic Race and came second to Alain Colas in the 70 foot (70 ft/21m) trimaran Pen Duick IV. Four years later Colas entered four masted Club Mediterranée (236 ft/72m), probably the largest boat ever sailed single-handed. He came second to Pen Duick IV sailed by Eric Tarbarly but time penalties because he needed help in raising sails pushed Colas back to fifth place. Ironically in the 1964 race the Pen Duick II (44 ft/13.5m) was condemned as too large for

one man to sail. Nowadays the upper limit for comfortable short-handed sailing is probably between 45–50 feet LOA.

Earlier, at the other end of the spectrum, Frank Dye showed what could be done in a Wayfarer dinghy with seamanlike passages to Iceland and Norway. Today, cruising Wayfarers are found everywhere and they are, by definition, short-handed. One of the very best small boat voyages was Allan Toone's 1978 Atlantic Circuit in a Corribee (21 ft/6.4m). He sailed 8,467 miles in 97 days, an average of over 87 miles per day in a boat with an 18-foot waterline! This is a truly astounding and largely unsung performance.

Excluding dinghies I would suggest that the lower size limit is between 18–20 feet LOA for

Yacht Motoring: motor sailers tend to be beamy and can make very comfortable cruising yachts provided their relatively poor windward performance under sail is acceptable.

A cruising Wayfarer Dinghy ...this one had just crossed the English Channel: Frank Dye sailed a Wayfarer to Norway. This one crossed the Channel with a crew of two who were living aboard in comfort.

no other reason that it is extremely difficult to fit a windvane self-steering system to a very small boat.

CONSTRUCTION MATERIAL

If you are planning to make modifications and intend to carry out the work yourself then it helps if the boat is built of a material that you have the skills to work. If you cannot weld then either learn how or do not buy a steel or aluminium hull. If you cannot laminate GRP,

Three yachts in Las Palmas preparing to cross the Atlantic to the Caribbean... the point here is the difference in size.

Twin Roller Jibs: this is the height of luxury for a cruising boat.

practise before trying it for real. If, like me, you can reduce an 8x4 inch sheet of plywood to sawdust in under 30 seconds and effortlessly strip the heads off screws, then do not buy a wooden boat. If you intend to cruise in the tropics, wooden hulls will need protection against teredo worm.

MODIFICATIONS ABOVE DECK

Type of Rig

Improving sail handling is one of the most important modifications. Once the conventional wisdom was that many sails make light work. Ketches, yawls, schooners, often cutter rigged, were a popular choice for the long-distance cruiser. The idea was to break the total sail area into a number of smaller sails, which were easier to handle than the large sails of a Bermudian rig. Occasionally the ability to rig twin-boomed headsails was built in. but in most cases sail handling meant a trip on deck regardless of the weather.

Modern sail handling challenged this thinking and won. Jester, of Transat fame, with its junk rig that could be handled from within the cabin, was an early example. For a time it looked as if this would become the rig of choice for the long-distance cruiser. Then came the likes of:

* Roller reefing head sails;
* In-mast mainsail reefing;
* In-boom mainsail reefing;

In-boom reefing.

- Snuffers for spinnakers;
- Slab reefing systems;
- Fully battened mainsails;
- Computer-controlled wing sails;
- Aero Rig;
- Freedom Rig.

They did not all appear at once and early examples were sometimes unreliable but they all aim take the pain out of sail handling and reduce the need to work on deck. Choice is a matter of personal preference but think carefully before making dramatic changes to the existing rig. Retro fitting in mast reefing is done but makes for a very broad mast compared to purpose designed system. Fitting an in-boom reefing system means a new boom. Changing a Bermudian rig to a ketch is a major undertaking but the work involved pales into insignificance if altering it to a junk rig.

It makes sense to opt for a system that requires the least alteration to your existing rig but unless you are prepared to call upon those off watch to help with sail handling then your choice system is directly related to the number of people on watch. If this is one person then you need a single-handed sail handling system.

Halyards

There is a tendency to accept unquestioningly that all halyards must be led aft to the cockpit. The reasoning behind this is that working on deck in a small boat is hazardous and should be reduced to a minimum. This is true only if the sails can be raised lowered and reefed from the cockpit. If you have, for example:

- hank on headsails;
- a main that will not drop by itself to be reefed;
- working at the mast to reef the main even if it does drop by itself;
- a spinnaker without a snuffer.

then you will need to go on deck to change headsails, reef the main, hoist, lower and recover the spinnaker. If the halyards for these sails are led aft to the cockpit then you face the dilemma of having to be in the cockpit to drop the sail while, at the same time, working at the mast or standing on the foredeck. When planning your halyard layout identify those that must stay on the mast.

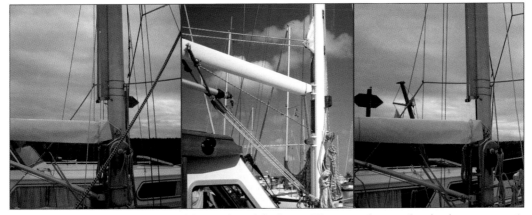

In-Mast Reefing: this system is an add on to the original mast. These are cheaper than buying a new mast with a dedicated in-mast reefing systems but add both weight and windage.

Slab reefing with lazy jacks: modern single-line slab reefing systems like this get rid of a lot of sail very quickly but are less versatile than a roller system. Sails often come with only two rows of reef points but every cruising boat should have a third, very deep, reef for really heavy weather.

Climbing the mast at sea is something to be avoided if at all possible. Whatever rig is chosen then all sails should have a spare halyard to reduce the need to replace a halyard at sea. Internal halyards are neater, but external halyards are easier to check and replace.

BOW ROLLERS

Cruising boats anchor not for lunch but for days at a time. On many modern yachts bow rollers, often little more than a fairlead, are pitiful. The idea that they would withstand the savage pitching and yawing at anchor in heavy weather is laughable and if your anchor fails you could find yourself on the beach. You may find it necessary to fit a much stronger bow roller that will take the inevitable abuse. You may also wish to fit a powered winch to help

Wing sail Las Palmas: this is a very high-tech solution to making sail handling easy. It is computer controlled and requires little input from the crew, provided the computer keeps working.

Wrecked Cat: if any link in your anchoring system from the anchor to the cleat onboard is suspect then you can end up on the beach.

Anchor and bow roller: anchors on cruising yachts should be oversized and the bow roller robust.

Samson Post: the crews of cruising boats often sleep when anchored and it is important that all fittings will withstand the inevitable abuse. Many fittings on many yachts are only designed to hold the yacht to a sheltered marina berth.

'Goalposts' on stern to carry equipment.

recover the anchor but remember these are power greedy. When upgrading the bow roller every other link in the chain between anchor and chain locker also needs to be upgraded. This includes the cleat or samson post used to secure the anchor. On many yachts these are good for a lunch break on a calm day but will not survive the yawing and pitching of being anchored in heavy weather.

GOALPOSTS

These are an increasingly popular way of carrying equipment like antennas. They normally have to be custom-made rather than bought off the shelf. They rarely come as standard.

SAFETY ON DECK

If a single-hander falls overboard then, miracles excepted, he is dead. If you are sailing short-handed the chances are better, perhaps as high as zero. Keep the crew aboard or, failing that, ensure they remain attached to the boat with the means of climbing back aboard.

When on deck it is important that when you put your foot down it stays there. Teak laid decks provide a good non-slip surface but many GRP decks have patches of moulded non-slip patterns alternating with areas of slippy, smooth gelcoat. This looks pretty but when the decks are wet the gelcoat is like ice and extraordinarily dangerous. Steel boats achieve the same effect with painted decks. You may not fall overboard but even a slip can be very painful. It is worth investing in good quality non-slip paint and covering the deck with it.

GRABRAILS

Grabrails may be a strip of wood which is fitted to small pillars moulded into the GRP deck. If the coachroof is curved to follow the shape of the hull then the line of the grabrail

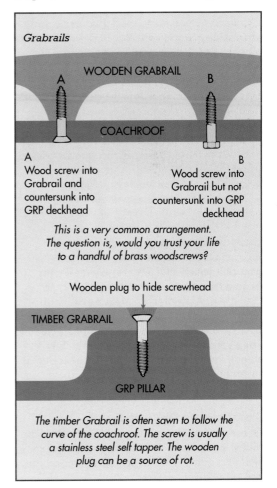

Grabrails

WOODEN GRABRAIL

COACHROOF

A
Wood screw into Grabrail and countersunk into GRP deckhead

B
Wood screw into Grabrail but not countersunk into GRP deckhead

This is a very common arrangement. The question is, would you trust your life to a handful of brass woodscrews?

Wooden plug to hide screwhead

TIMBER GRABRAIL

GRP PILLAR

The timber Grabrail is often sawn to follow the curve of the coachroof. The screw is usually a stainless steel self tapper. The wooden plug can be a source of rot.

will follow this curve. Ideally the wood should
have been steamed and bent to the curve but
it is more likely to have been sawn, which
significantly reduces its strength as the grain
of the wood no longer follows the curve.
A very common arrangement is a strip of
timber with handholds cut out at intervals
and attached directly to the deck.
In both cases the grabrails are held on to the
deck by woodscrews. The worst example I
have seen was of self-tapping screws into
GRP! I have never heard of a case of grabrails
failing but I mistrust screws to take the weight
of a falling crew member.

Ideally grabrails should be bolted through the
coachroof but as the timber is often no more
than 15–20mm (occasionally 25mm) wide
there are problems fitting a decent sized bolt.
A 5mm bolt is probably the absolute minimum
and that would leave around 10mm of wood
either side. Would you trust 10mm of timber to
take the shock of an adult being thrown at it?
Allowing for the cut of the threads a 5mm is
effectively a 3mm rod. You can bend 3mm rod
between your fingers. It is the devil and deep
blue sea. There are three options:

*Rollbar over pramhood: pramhoods are often used
as handholds when going on deck to handle sails.
The fitting for most pramhoods are not strong
enough to be used as a handhold. This is a good,
safe alternative.*

- Increase the size of the bolt and accept this
  reduces the thickness of the wood on either
  side.
- Fit bigger and stronger grabrails.
- Regard the grabrails as decorative
  features.

Size of Grabrails
Before holding on to a small and skimpy
grabrail, you must first carefully feed your
fingers through a gap only slightly bigger
than the average hand. This is a challenge
when wearing gloves. It is much better to
have grabrails you can slap your hand on and
wrap your fingers around in a death defying
grip. If I want to clip my safety harness into a
grabrail I want to be able to do so quickly, in
the dark and one handed.

Positioning Grabrails
Grabrails are normally located on coachroofs
and you take hold by either leaning over or
bending down or both. In either position you
are out of balance. Grabrails should be

located so that you can catch hold standing
upright with all your weight travelling directly
through your feet so you can brace yourself
with your arms. This may be nit picking but
safety for the short-handed sailor depends on
paying attention to small risks rather than
obvious death delivering dangers.

I stumbled upon my ideal grabrails. I saw a
yacht with a stainless steel tube running across
the cockpit, above and following the line of the
sprayhood. It looked like sport's car roll bar. I
know a good idea when I see one. Not only did
it provide protection against the boom
dropping suddenly dropping down but it was
the ideal handhold when entering or leaving the
cockpit. I was in the habit of hanging onto the
sprayhood as I left the cockpit to go forward
and had nightmares about going over the side
with the sprayhood in my hand.

To be really secure an rollbar must be supported fore or aft providing this was the opportunity of dispensing with the original wooden grabrails and replacing them with large diameter, easy-to-reach stainless steel tubing port and starboard. The whole arrangement is fixed to the coachroof with 10mm and 12mm bolts running through large backing pads. Unkind critics say that if it fails then it takes the coachroof with it. It is not to everyone's taste but I like it.

JACKSTAYS

Jackstays are lines running port and starboard the entire length of the boat. The idea is that you clip your harness into them before leaving the cockpit and remain clipped in until you return to the cockpit. If you do fall overboard you remain attached to the boat. This may not be ideal but it is better than swimming. A single jackstay on the centre line lessens the distance you fall and allows you to lean back to steady yourself when you are working, but your safety line can interfere with sheets and halyards.

Some prefer wire jackstays. These rattle and roll around the deck and from inside the cabin sound like a demented drummer. The noise can be lessened by using plastic-covered wire but the plastic can hide faults in the wire. I prefer rope. Jackstays should be renewed each season and whenever they are subjected to a shock loading.

SAFETY HARNESS STRONG POINTS

Make lots of strong points where a safety line can be clipped in. It should be possible to clip into a cockpit strong point before leaving the cabin and when finished working on deck to remain clipped in until safely back in the cabin. You should always be able to reach two anchor points so that you never unclip from one before clipping into another. Every anchor point must have decent backing pads to spread the load throughout the hull or deck. Anchor points must never be shared. Everyone in the cockpit needs their own harness anchor point. In really horrible weather you may wish to clip into two anchor points just to be sure of staying with the boat should one fail.

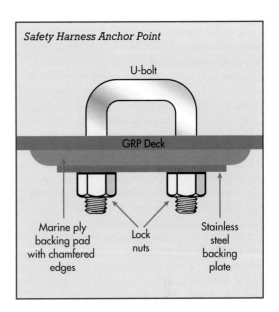

Safety Harness Anchor Point

U-bolt

GRP Deck

Marine ply backing pad with chamfered edges

Lock nuts

Stainless steel backing plate

GRANNY BARS

On larger boats granny bars around the mast are a good idea. They look like zimmer frames and increase windage, but they do improve safety when you are working at the mast, and investing in self-tailing winches allows you to hoist sails and keep one hand free for holding on.

GUARDRAILS

Guardrails are a menace. They are good for hanging out washing, holding up netting, dodgers and fenders, but little else. They catch the average adult behind the knees as he falls overboard and they are a huge obstacle to climbing back aboard. Side decks on small yachts are often no more than four or five inches wide except where they are blocked by chainplate fittings. When you go forward the choice is between:

- shuffling along stuck between the guardrail and the side of the coachroof. For much of the way the guardrails are more of a hindrance than a safety feature. It is slow work, and most of the time you are off balance.
- climbing outside the guard rails to leave the cockpit and then back over when you reach the foredeck. For the greater part of your journey you are outside the guardrails.

If your boat has narrow sidedecks it puts a question mark on the value of fitting guardrails. Round the cockpit they provide a convenient backrest and somewhere to hang dodgers but forward of the cockpit I am not sure they serve any useful purpose especially when roller-reefing headsails have reduced the need to go forward and you no longer have to lash headsails to the pulpit. Many years ago I was aboard a Scania 40 taking part in the Round Zealand Race. There were no guardrails, or for that matter, pushpit or pulpit. The crew were keen, the skipper keener and sail changes were frequent. Having never sailed without guardrails I found then prospect of going forward daunting but by the end of three days I was charging along the side deck and throwing myself into the sail with the rest of the deck apes.

Margo's sidedecks are about four inches wide and whenever I went forward I seemed to spend all my time clipping and unclipping my lifeline from the jackstay as I climbed over the guardrails. It was slow, dangerous and once cost me a spinnaker pole. Finally, as I upgraded the grabrails, I removed the guardrails between cockpit and the pulpit and found I could move around quickly and safely.

SELF-STEERING
Very few yachts will steer themselves on any point of sail for long periods. I know of only one and that was a replica of *Spray*. There are arrangements of bungees and sheets which claim to steer boats. I have tried a few and none have worked better or longer than lashing the helm. Some commercial helm-lashing systems promise you can leave the helm for short periods. I am sure that their claims are true but I would doubt their efficiency with fin and skeg or fin and spade rudder designs. I would expect them to work best on long-keeled yachts and then only when the boat is either close hauled or reaching. This is when these boats are easily steered by balancing the sails. Why buy something your boat does for free?

Except for very short passages, completed within a couple of hours, some form of reliable self-steering is essential otherwise navigation, sail handling, eating, resting and life in general

Monitor Self-Steering gear.

becomes difficult. Helming for long periods, say over ten hours at a stretch is possible but it is very demanding and steering a compass course throughout the night induces a trance like state where your mind roams the oceans of planet Zen. Fitting a dependable self-steering gear is high on the list of essential modifications.

Types of Self-Steering
Self-steering systems are either wind powered, which steer courses relative to the wind, or electronic, which steer a compass course. Most electronic units can fit a sensor which will steer a course relative to the wind, and some sailors jury rig an arrangement which links their wind vane to an electronic unit so that it can hold a compass course.

Types of Wind Vane Self-Steering
Wind vanes are either vertically or horizontally pivoted. In the early days all vanes were

Mintaka at Matinique... Plastimo Self-Steering.

Rail as Cleat... Windpilot self-steering.

vertically pivoted vanes and worked on the same principle as a church weathercock. Size meant power. In the first OSTAR, Chichester had a brute the size of a mizzen sail called Miranda, on Gipsy Moth II. It worked in theory and gave him no end of grief.

Nowadays nearly all vanes are horizontally pivoted which means they weathercock when they stand upright and fall over to port or starboard when the wind strikes them from the side. Horizontally pivoted vanes are more sensitive and powerful than vertically pivoted vanes, so much so that for a time it was thought that the vane alone had enough power to steer the boat. This promised cheap, cheerful self-steering fitted with the minimum of adaptation to your boat. For a couple of seasons I sailed with one hanging from the pushpit and, to be fair, it worked in a gale but at other times tended to be workshy. They are rarely seen nowadays.

It is far better to use the vane as a sensor and link it to a paddle. As long as the vane remains vertical the paddle stays on the fore and aft line of the boat. If the vane falls over to one side or another then the paddle turns just like a small rudder and the water rushing past it causes it to swing up to one side. This pendulum effect pulls lengths of line attached to the helm, which hauls the boat back on course and brings the vane back upright. This is the servo pendulum system. *Jester* had one in the first OSTAR. They are extremely powerful and reliable.

A variation is to stop the paddle penduluming and treat it as an auxiliary rudder. It need not be very big, for the main ship's rudder can be used as a trim tab and remove all weather or lee helm to reduce the loads on the auxiliary rudder. Auxiliary rudders are good on centre cockpit boats where the stretch and friction on the long control lines from the vane to the wheel seriously reduces a servo pendulum's efficiency.

Another approach is to link the vane to a trim tab on the main rudder. The vane turns the trim tab one way. The rudder turns to come in line with the trim tab and this steers the boat back on course. These are not as popular as servo-pendulums or auxiliary rudders and work best on boats with transom hung rudders.

There are many variations on these three principal types of wind vane. For example, the Navik uses a trim tab on a servo-pendulum system. This allows it to use a smaller, less obtrusive vane. It works well. I sailed thousands of miles with one. Windpilot have a combined servo-pendulum and auxiliary rudder.

Fitting a Windvane

Fitting a windvane is not always easy. With a transom-hung rudder the entire system has to be placed outboard of the rudder. This means attaching some form of bracket to the stern to carry the self-steering. Davits have to go, or at the very least, the dinghy they are meant to carry is stowed elsewhere. Boarding ladders must be offset to port or starboard or removed entirely and some form of bracket is necessary on sugar scoop sterns. There is no easy answer to a mizzen with its boom extending over the transom. Even if the boom manages to clear the vane then the wind spilling off the sail can confuse the vane.

Some multihulls can be steered using a windvane but not only are there problems linking the vane to the tiller(s) or wheel, but on the faster multihulls variations in wind speed and the resultant changes in boat speed means constant changes in relative wind direction which the wind vane follows. It is more usual to fit an electronic autohelm.

Types of Electronic Self-Steering

Electronic self-steering systems are much easier to fit. They steer a course relative to their internal compass. Once that was all, but nowadays they can be interfaced with the GPS and plotter and will steer the boat from start to finish with no further input from the crew. There are push-pull types for tiller steered yachts, the belt type for wheel steered yachts, and more powerful hydraulic systems for either wheel- or tiller-steered yachts.

Electronic systems are very reliable but the more powerful they are the better they work and the more they cost. Always choose the most powerful unit you can afford.

A major drawback of electronic systems is that despite electronic wizardry to minimise consumption they are power greedy and the engine (or generator) must be run regularly to keep the batteries topped up. Solar panels and wind generators are unlikely to provide sufficient power to run autohelms continuously.

COMFORT ON DECK

Even sitting in the cockpit keeping a lookout, runs the risk of becoming tired, cold and wet. It is possible to suffer from any two of these miseries at the same time and still remain operational. It will not be fun and there is a very definite limit on how long you can continue before you begin running on residual adrenaline.

Being cold, wet and tired simultaneously finishes you within minutes. Hypothermia does not announce its arrival, it creeps up unnoticed. You start shivering, you become drowsy, and less and less aware of what is happening around you. Actions become instinctive rather than rational, and then irrational. Finally, you stop shivering and drift into unconsciousness. Not once during all this has it occurred to you that you are suffering from hypothermia. Fatigue increases susceptibility and to the single-hander, hypothermia is a greater danger than a lee shore in a gale.

Avoidance is better than cure. Give some thought on how to maximise the opportunities for staying rested, warm and dry. The first rule

is to protect yourself from the weather as much as possible. Spend as much time below as is consistent with safety. On deck always wear good oilskins and lots of warm clothing. Always wear a hat. Have a selection of towels or scarves to keep water from running down your neck. When one becomes wet then replace it. Rig some form of shelter in the cockpit. This usually takes the form of a pramhood cuddy or wheelhouse which along with dodgers keeps you out of most of the weather most of the time.

SAFETY EQUIPMENT

Lifebuoys, danbuoys and floating lights are not much use to the single-handed sailor but most seem to carry them. The safety requirements of the short-handed sailor are no different from any other sailor but he is probably more aware of safety issues as there are fewer people around to make good any errors he makes.

Man Overboard

Wear a harness and clip in all the time. If you have fitted jackstays, have lots of harness anchor points and good non-slip decks, then you have reduced the odds of falling overboard to a minimum. You should be able to move around the cockpit and deck in comparative safety. If you do go overboard then you will remain attached to the boat and the challenge will be climbing back aboard.

Fear does not give you superhuman strength. Unless you are young, and very fit you will not have the upper body strength to haul yourself back aboard. A more likely scenario is that you will be less than fit, overweight, the water will be cold, and you will be wearing oilskins over fleeces and jumpers. Within seconds, your once warm and now cold, sodden clothing will have doubled or trebled your body weight.

You must act quickly before the cold wins. You will have time to make no more than two or three attempts to climb aboard before exhaustion sets in and are reduced to going through the motions, knowing that you have lost but refusing to give up. Without a ready-made plan and the means to implement it, climbing back aboard may be impossible.

Legs are more powerful than arms so the first priority is take your weight off your arms and put it onto to your feet. If you can extend this principle and contrive a ladder it becomes possible to clamber up it and back aboard. I have got into the habit of sailing with foot loops spaced port and starboard around the deck. The idea is, should I fall overboard, to haul myself along the jackstay until I could reach one of these loops, pull it down, stand in it and make another loop out of the second safety line on my harness and climb aboard. It works alongside the pontoon.

What I would do if I could not reach one of my pre-positioned loops? Part of my mast-climbing apparatus is an etrier, a souvenir from my climbing days. An etrier is a short ladder used in artificial climbing. Early models were made of rope with metal or wooden rungs but later models were made out of tape which was more secure, for the tape wraps round your boot making almost impossible for it to slip out. Etriers are light and with a snaplink in either end I could clip it into my harness, hang it round my neck and carry my emergency boarding ladder with me as I moved around the deck. I could even use it as a spare safety line. If I did fall overboard then all I have to do is reach up and clip it into the jackstay running along the side deck, and I would have a boarding ladder exactly where I needed it.

In the real world not everyone clips in all the time. I don't and it is stupid. I lost a perfectly good spinnaker pole north of the Cape Verde Islands because I had a choice of dropping it overboard and grabbing the rail, or falling overboard with the pole. It was an easy decision but what can you do if you fall overboard without being attached to the boat?

The honest answer is not a lot. The chances of swimming fast enough to overhaul a yacht are remote. Alain Bombard when crossing the Atlantic in his inflatable *Heritique* became becalmed and went for a swim. The wind returned and he only just made it back to his raft. He was an Olympic-class swimmer. Some believe in towing a knotted line astern so that if they fall overboard they have a chance of grabbing it and pulling themselves back to the

boat although a line rigged to disconnect the self-steering and bring the boat up into the wind and stop it may be better. Both suggestions assume you have the wits and the time to reach the line before it sails out of reach. They are really forlorn hopes. It is far better to always wear a harness and use it.

BELOW-DECK MODIFICATIONS

A tired, uncomfortable crew is likely to make errors. Can you live a civilised life on the boat? Can it be modified so you can live, not camp aboard? Staying rested and comfortable is important and adds immensely to the enjoyment of a passage.

A boat should be snug, relaxing and easy to live in below decks. Tasks like navigating, cooking, sitting, sleeping or even moving around should not be physically difficult or require any abnormal effort. Can you work comfortably at the navigation table in any weather by day and night? On one boat I had you had to stand up to work at the chart table. I held on with one hand and plotted with the other. On another boat I could cook on one tack but not navigate, and on the other tack, navigate but not cook.

Can you cook in any weather? The cook must have both hands free, be secure and not be thrown around when boat moves. Simply wedging yourself in a corner is not good enough. At some point you will be flung out, probably when you are holding a pot of boiling water. Cooking needs a gimballed stove with pot holders and sensible, easy access ready-to-use stowage for food, pots, pans and plates.

When a meal is cooked can you eat it in comfort? Eating an all in mess out of a dog bowl may sound rugged and adventurous. It sustains life but that is all that can be said in its favour. On a passage of any length meals are a highlight of the day so forever serving up something that looks like it has been scraped off your seaboot points up the value of cooking proper meals and tucking into a decent meal whatever the weather.

Are there bunks you can sleep in in any weather, at any angle of heel? Many boats have master cabins with large, comfortable double bunks, which are marvellous for entertaining in harbour and next to useless at sea. What is required on passage are seaberths with easy to release lee cloths or boards so you can rush on deck when needed. Can you use the heads on either tack in any weather? The alternative does not bear thinking about.

Safe movement below decks needs lots of grabrails around the cabin(s) so you always have something to hang on to as the boat rocks and rolls. This is necessary even on small yachts. Big waves, especially those running across the dominant wave front, can toss the boat about in unexpected ways. They mean no harm and are no danger to the boat but they toss people across the cabin and the resulting damage ranges from bumps and sprains to broken limbs, back and head injuries. When working out where to place grabrails below, adopt the principle of always being able to reach the next grabrail before letting go of the first. The provision of grabrails below decks on most production boats ranges from none at all to completely inadequate.

Electronic navigation has reduced the importance of the traditional navigation area. The requirement now is vertical space to display instruments rather than room to work on a chart. Gadgets make navigation a breeze but can you see, in detail, all you wish on a computer generated chart? What if the instruments fail? Is there still space to stow paper charts? And room to work on them? If not then think about clipping the chart to a board and working with it on your knee. When not needed, the board can be stowed under a bunk mattress.

When the single-handed sailor enters harbours or anchorages the demands of navigation conflict with those of boat handling. Often you need to be simultaneously in the cockpit and at the chart table. The answer is bring the chart into the cockpit, and a good solution is the wooden board under the bunk. Clip the chart to it and stow it under the pramhood until it is needed. It helps night navigation if you rig up a small red light under the pramhood so that you can look at the chart with both hands free.

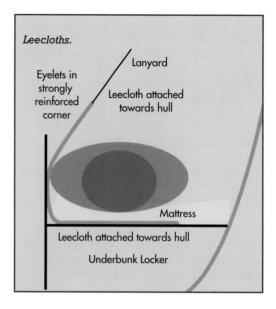

Leecloths.

Eyelets in strongly reinforced corner

Lanyard

Leecloth attached towards hull

Mattress

Leecloth attached towards hull

Underbunk Locker

Stowage

At some time you will be faced with the dilemma of searching for some item you know for certain is aboard but you cannot remember where it is stowed. Locker after locker is unpacked. The cabin sole is a clutter of gear that threatens to bury you every time the boat rolls. It is impossible to move about the cabin without shifting several tons of kit and the knowledge that it all has to be restowed does nothing to sweeten your mood. Searching lockers at night holding a torch in your teeth adds to the fun.

One solution is to number off every locker, however small, and in a looseleaf book using one page per locker list the contents of each locker. It is important to keep this list up to date. This is easy for lockers containing non-perishable items like toolkits and spares whose contents will change slowly if at all but for lockers holding consumables like food and fuel then you will need spare sheets to keep them up to date.

It takes time and a certain amount of self-discipline to keep the stowage book up to date but besides making it easy to lay your hand on any item of kit when you need it, it is worth its weight in gold when you are preparing for a passage, for it highlights shortages to be made good before casting off.

CHECKLIST MODIFICATIONS TO STANDARD CRUISER TO IMPROVE SHORT-HANDED SAILING

ABOVE DECK HELMING	Guardrails	RIG	BELOW DECKS
Self-steering	Granny bars at mast	Roller-reefing	Navigation area
Electronic	Non-slip deck	headsail(s)	Instrumentation
Windvane	Boarding loops	Mainsail reefing	Sea berths
Tiller extension	Radar reflector	Halyard arrangement	Galley
	Radar Target		Gimball stove
	enhancer	COCKPIT	Ready-to-use stowage
SAFETY	Radar Detector	INSTRUMENTS	Grab rails
Anchor points for		Visibility	Number off lockers
safety harnesses	COMFORT	By day	
Jackstays	Pramhood/dog house	By night	
Grab rails	Dodgers		

Lockers and other stowage are classed as:
a. Ready to Use Stowage that it is easily accessible in all weathers without digging under bunks or shifting several tons of equipment to find the item you wish. Ready-to-use stowage includes items such as:
- Food and water for two or three days;
- Oilskins, lifejackets and harnesses;
- Immediate first aid…mostly sticking plasters, antiseptic creams, mild pain killers and seasickness remedies along with any personal medication you may be taking;
- Emergency tool kit of hammer, knife, adjustable spanner, mole grips, screwdrivers, torches.

b. Deep Stowage This is fairly accessible stowage, usually in underbunk lockers where some unpacking is required to reach the desired item(s) but not an excessive amount. Deep stowage will be accessed every few days mostly to replenish the consumables in the ready to use stowage.
c. Long Term This is for items that will only be needed very occasionally. Reaching items in it is a major operation and often requires unpacking entire lockers to find a single item.

While the amount and contents of the ready to use stowage are pretty much the same regardless of length of voyage, deep stowage and long-term stowage will vary depending on the time you expect to be at sea. A long passage requires more rations and equipment and the number and type of spares carried will be in inverse proportion to your access to repair and maintenance facilities.

A dedicated wet locker is essential. When not being worn, oilskins should be in the wet locker otherwise the cabin will become a damp pit. If there is no wet locker then fix hooks in the heads and hang your oilskins there.

A wise yachtsman has tools for all occasions stowed in a tool box and buried deep in the bosun's locker. This is fine for planned or major maintenance but too inaccessible for small running repairs. A screwdriver (with a selection of blades), knife, pliers and an adjustable spanner are sufficient for most day-to-day repairs. Stow them where they can be easily reached.

Using the all the points covered in this chapter as an aide memoire allows you to produce a schedule of modifications for your boat. No two lists should be the same. How you rig the boat, your living arrangements and the level of equipment needed should reflect the sailing you want to do, what equipment you already have, and what work you believe is necessary.

Do not make modifications for their own sake. Rely on you own judgement, not adverts. Listen to others but remember no one's opinions are gospel and may not always be backed by relevant experience or knowledge. Test you proposals against the KISS (Keep It Simple Stupid) principle and discard any that do not make this standard. If gear can fail then it will. Unnecessarily complicated modifications or equipment are most likely to pack up when you need them most.

3 The Skipper

Preparing your boat for short-handed sailing can dominate thinking and completely obscure that it is equally important to equip you, the skipper, with the skills necessary to command the short- or single-handed yacht. Seamanship is a given but it is only one of the skills required.

Practical Skills

Every skipper ought to have some knowledge of how every single facet of their boat functions. This seems obvious but this is normally shared amongst those onboard. Usually amongst the crew there is someone who understands the working of diesel engines. There will be someone who is initiated into the mysteries of electrics and electronics and at least one person aboard keen to play the amateur weather forecaster. There will be those whose only interest is sails and sail trimming, or navigating or cooking.

For many years I sailed with an expert mechanic and my knowledge of marine engines still barely extends beyond stopping and starting. Although I can talk knowledgably about engine revolutions and oil pressure, my words mean very little to me and probably less to anyone listening. For a while I had a superb tactician aboard and when confronted with a sail handling or trimming problem my contribution was confined to asking, 'What do you think we should do?' Many skippers sail with only the faintest understanding of what makes their boat tick. There is not a criticism. You may be a master in every skill and lack the leadership qualities necessary to be a skipper.

SKIPPERING SKILLS

PRACTICAL SKILL	THEORETICAL SKILL
Navigator	Planner
Tactician	If not an 'action man' then a 'doer' able to put theory and plans into action.
Weather Forecaster	Resolute and determined
Helmsman	Leader
Sail trimmer	Trainer
Bosun	Pupil, always learning, if only from his/her own mistakes
Carpenter	Self-disciplined
Welder	Self-reliant
Laminator	Motivator
Mechanical and electrical engineer	Self-confident
Electronic engineer	Realist
Sailmaker	Critic or assessor of his and others' performance
Radio ham	Judge of people, including him/herself
Computer operator	Manager of people and him/herself
Cook	Taker of calculated risks
First aider	A curious dreamer

If you only sail short-handed occasionally or limit your activities to short day passages and rely upon shore-based specialist help to maintain your boat you may not be aware of how little you know. I did not know the scale of my ignorance. Imagine something as simple as a fuel blockage. I find bleeding the fuel supply of a diesel engine a horrible task and although it is not difficult I am always surprised when it works. The ability to perform such simple tasks could be the difference between declaring an emergency and carrying on under your own power.

The short-handed skipper is a jack of all trades. It is unlikely that any individual will be expert in every skill, and not all skills are of equal importance. Most electronic equipment is probably beyond amateur probing but even a low-level understanding of electronic circuitry and how it works can prove invaluable. If you plan to sail beyond the reach of the local chandlers then it would be prudent to acquire at least a basic level of competence in most skills before setting out.

Some skills, like navigating, require a sound theoretical knowledge backed up by many sea miles and aeons of sea time before true competence appears. For other skills a basic competence is acquired by attending the appropriate course and, with luck, this will be sufficient see you through difficulties until you can reach qualified assistance. Some courses are run under the umbrella of the RYA, others like electronics, welding or computing will be found at your local FE College as either part or full time courses, and some are run by organisations such as the Red Cross or St John's Ambulance Brigade. Putting in the sea miles and going on courses is all part of the practical passage planning. You will be amazed at the range of courses offered by your local FE College. Ignorance, as I learned the hard way, is an explanation, not an excuse.

The gaps in your skill base will reflect your inclinations. You may be an eager radio ham, in which case radios and electronics will hold no terrors but you may have only the barest understanding on how to hand,

reef and steer. You may be a staunch traditionalist, regard all modern gadgetry as unnecessary and sail with nothing more than a chart, a compass, a wind-up watch and cook on a Rippingill stove. If so, then digital charts and GPS will be a mystery. It does not matter. What is important is that you have made a careful inventory of your practical abilities, reviewed the gamut of electrical, mechanical and nautical misfortunes that can befall your boat and are happy that you are capable of making a decent stab at dealing with any problem that may arise with the resources on board. If not, then you must fill the gaps. The lowest acceptable standard is the ability to make get-you-home repairs. There is no disgrace in being a good bodger. You are looking for a successful solution, not perfection.

THEORETICAL SKILLS

I am unsure how to define the theoretical skills the short-handed skipper should have except to say that although he must practise them they are not practical in a hands on hammer-bashing manner.

Passage Planning

Planning comes high on the list. According to my grandmother a planner is someone who, having learnt the lessons of history, uses them to write horoscopes. Few plans survive contact with reality but without a plan there is no framework on how to deal with the unexpected.

Passage planning is a good example. Skippers of fully crewed boats can delegate the various elements of passage planning amongst his crew but the short-handed sailor must do the work himself and if you have set a firm date for departure there is a real danger that you will sail with the planning and preparation incomplete. The history of short-handed sailing is littered with hurried departures, boats sailing with work unfinished and stores strewn haphazardly over the cabin.

Setting out, even in the best of conditions and for the shortest of passages, is demanding. You are in busy waters and dangers abound. You will not have found your sea legs or fallen into a comfortable routine. Nothing is properly stowed. You are uncertain if all supplies are aboard, the passage plan is incomplete and the radio has just announced a gale warning. The skill in preparing for a voyage is planning, so that all falls into its place at the right time. Passage planning is time consuming, hard work often without any immediate results when other work is clamouring for your attention. To be sure it is properly complete you must begin planning earlier than you first think and make allowance for the inevitable delays.

Selecting The Crew

Another theoretical skill is being a judge of people, including yourself. If you sail with your family there is no choice of crew but when sailing with friends the smart skipper tries to select a crew whose strengths will complement each other, whose weaknesses are known but can be overlooked and who will all live happily together. He must also assess his own strengths and weaknesses and those of the crew in the light of the passage they are about undertake.

Single-handed sailors must question themselves and answer in the knowledge that they have no one to rely upon but themselves. They alone must carry the full burden of workload, decision-making and responsibility. It is best they give honest answers.

Is the passage well within their past experience? If not then in what respects is it different? Are these differences significant? Have they the skills to cope with these differences? Are they pushing the performance envelope of themselves or their boat beyond sensible limits?

These questions are not arguments for always sailing within your known limits. Experience comes from sailing beyond your present boundaries of skill and knowledge but you must decide if the balance between the known and unknown is too far out of kilter. There is a difference between testing your ability and not knowing what you are doing. The first is stretching your limits and the other is plain stupid but do not mistake the nervousness

that should accompany the start of every voyage for 'No'. For me the final question is, 'Will I have fun?'

I was in Falmouth preparing to sail to La Coruña and used the excuse of waiting for the right weather to delay sailing. Truth was I had not decided if I could manage the passage. Till then my longest short-handed passage had been under 150 miles. Now I was intending to more than double it. In addition I had to cross some of the world's busiest shipping lanes. For much of the way I would be off soundings, and ahead lay Biscay, famous for devouring ships. I was doing it in a Hurley 20. If I ran into trouble, critics would queue up to point out that I had chosen the wrong boat for this passage. I sailed with my heart in my mouth, had an enjoyable passage and redrew the boundaries of my experience.

Managing The Crew

Every skipper, short-handed or not must look after the crew. Crew management means ensuring everyone on board has a safe, comfortable and enjoyable voyage. It is a cross between man management and mothering. This is still true even if you are sailing alone. You must make adequate arrangements to look after yourself, no one else will, and the attitude that 'I'll manage somehow' is an invitation trouble gladly accepts. Introducing and enforcing watch-keeping systems, observing safety procedures (like wearing harnesses) and keeping to the daily routine are important. So too is a good watch-keeping system. A bad watch system on a crewed boat still gives everybody fairly long rest periods but for the short-handed it is sailing into trouble.

Skippers of crewed yachts delegate duties as part of their overall management strategy. The short-handed sailor learns to prioritise. This is much more demanding. Not only must you decide on what has to be done, you have to calculate the best order in which to carry out individual tasks. Sometimes it is impossible to avoid conflicting priorities and like the juggler spinning plates on sticks you rush from one task to the next. The ability to multi-task is

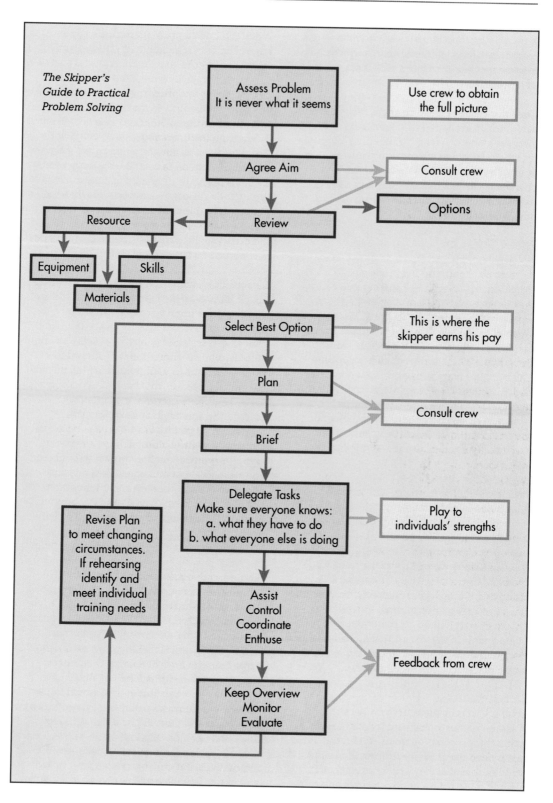

The Skipper's Guide to Practical Problem Solving

Assess Problem
It is never what it seems

Use crew to obtain the full picture

Agree Aim

Consult crew

Review

Options

Resource

Equipment

Skills

Materials

Select Best Option

This is where the skipper earns his pay

Plan

Consult crew

Brief

Delegate Tasks
Make sure everyone knows:
a. what they have to do
b. what everyone else is doing

Play to individuals' strengths

Revise Plan to meet changing circumstances. If rehearsing identify and meet individual training needs

Assist
Control
Coordinate
Enthuse

Feedback from crew

Keep Overview
Monitor
Evaluate

knowing how long you may spend on one task before the plates start tumbling, and which task must be tackled next. It is a skill that improves with practice.

Consider beating into a strange, busy harbour at night. You are faced with working out how long each board should be, keeping a lookout for other shipping (and working out what it is doing), trying to make sense of shore and channel lights, ticking off the buoys as you pass them, checking the chart from time to time, and helming.

Crew Training

No one should be given a task they cannot or know not how to do but it happens. Confidence comes from knowing you can do what is asked. This applies to the short-handed sailor as well as his crew. Do not set yourself or anyone else a task without first making sure you, or they, have the skills to complete it. If not, arrange the appropriate training. This may be a shore-based course or five minutes on-board instruction. When teaching someone a practical skill the sequence of instruction is: you demonstrate the skill, they imitate until they have it right and then they practise until they do it right every time.

Training includes learning, actively seeking out gaps in the information you require and trying to fill them. It may be as simple as a lack of local knowledge. This can be made good by buying the appropriate yachting pilot or better still, speaking to local sailors. I was in *Riddle of the Sands* country where passages follow a rising tide along drying channels, and my pilot described my choice of route as a 'classic'. On the chart it looked straightforward but in the yacht club I learned that all had changed. Even at high water the channel had less than a metre of water. I went another way.

Leadership

Leadership is management under stress. A leader enthuses his team by example to achieve their common goals. When the going is easy and the answers obvious leaders are so numerous that they are on special offer and often it is a case of buy one get one free.

When difficulties arise, leaders are scarce. It is surprising how many people stand around waiting to be told what to do. A leader is, or appears to be, in control of the situation and creates order and direction in uncertain and unknown situations. He makes decisions without referring to others. This is not the same as ignoring the crew and issuing commands. Nor does it mean that the skipper lets the crew take a vote and does what the majority want. It means the skipper hears what the crew have to say, then makes his decision. He then works out how to implement it, explains his plan to the crew, rehearses if necessary, and then he and the crew put the plan into action. Giving orders is replaced by sharing out tasks.

By consulting with his crew, the skipper has a check placed on his more outrageous ideas and can draw upon the expertise within the crew to flesh out his proposals. Having allocated tasks so that they play to the strengths of individual crew members he knows that when he comes to implement his plan he has the enthusiastic approval and support of his crew. This alone can take the skipper's confidence into orbit. Self-confidence, misplaced or not, real or faked can make an indifferent plan successful. Inexperienced skippers working on the edge of their ability are more likely to make mistakes through uncertainty, nervousness and a tendency to do nothing before they have found the perfect answer. Dominated by their worries, unsure what to do next and with their crew asking, 'What do we do now?' their leadership suffers.

Single-handed sailors have no one but themselves to restrain their more outrageous ideas, no expertise but their own to call upon and the confidence that they have selected the best option from all those that he can see comes from within. The accounts of the great short-handers from Slocum to Chichester, David Lewis and Knox Johnson all tell how when they had a problem they would think about it carefully, sometimes for days, make up their mind and then act. And that is the key. Think the problem through and when you have decided on a course of action, forget the alternatives and concentrate all your energy and assets on making your choice work rather than wasting time and resources wondering if you have missed the one right answer. Your plan, promptly and well executed is far better than sitting around waiting for the best plan to pop into your head.

There is no guarantee that your plan will work. Rank has its privileges and one of them is making mistakes and carrying the can. Every skipper must accept full accountability for his decisions and their consequences. No one else is to blame if a plan goes wrong. Crews, even when they have erred, object to being used as excuses for what they regard as the skipper's mistakes. This does not prevent skippers salving their ego by publicly accepting responsibility while privately blaming the crew.

Single-handed sailors do not have the comfort of secretly believing the mess they have created is really someone else's fault. There is no question over who is to blame and accepting the consequences of your incompetence, carelessness or plain downright stupidity can be like one of those tortures the Greek gods were fond of inflicting on their heroes. You brood. Replay events time and time again wondering where you (or fickle fate) went wrong. This is not learning from your mistakes, it is worrying them to death, and left unchecked, this behaviour can erode self-confidence to the point of immobility when you next encounter some difficulty. It turns molehills into high mountain ranges and perfectly natural concerns into full-blown panic attacks. Constantly thinking about past failures wastes time that could be better used putting present problems right.

Self-discipline

When the going gets tough the skipper knows that times will become much rougher if he allows his behaviour to convey his concerns to the crew. He may be worried to death and on the edge of panic but as long as he looks cheerful, speaks slowly and keeps his voice down the chances are his crew will not notice anything is wrong, or if they do, decide that it is not worth worrying about as it is obvious that the skipper is unconcerned. It is a weird symbiosis. The presence of the crew forces the skipper to keep his cool and because the

skipper is outwardly calm the crew do not worry. This alone can save the day.

The single-hander has no cause to maintain a front but even more reason to control his concerns. As some point concerns shade into fears, fears into panic and panic into despair. If you curl up into a ball and begin sucking your thumb there is no one else ready and eager to produce a captain's cap from their sea bag, take over and save the day. There is no formula for single-handed panic control. It is very personal. Some folk let their fears out by hurling imprecations at the heavens even as they tackle the problem. Others promise to lead pure and perfect lives in return for celestial assistance or bottle up their worries and fears and act as though life is normal until the crisis is over when they collapse from delayed terror. A few become excited, hyped up and revel in their flirtation with danger. Whatever form your panic control takes it is important that you recognise the earliest signs of fear and bring it under control long before it takes control of you.

The Motivator

A good skipper and crew motivate each other in the same way that they feed off each other to control their fears. The skipper encourages the crew to perform well and a good performance by the crew gives confidence to the skipper.

Skippers must reassure their crews in order to develop their self-confidence, self-reliance, and encourage the belief that they are controlling events rather than vice versa. They should promote social interaction between crew members in order to build up teamwork so that each crew member can rely upon support from others. Everyone should be fully in the picture all of the time so that they understand where their tasks fit into the wider scheme of things.

The single-handed sailor must be self-motivating which is far harder. For me the best way is setting achievable goals. I try not to look at the voyage as a whole (I find this can be daunting) but only as far as my next port. If that is not possible then I aim for the next waypoint or some other close-to-hand milestone. I often see if I can better yesterday's mileage. Having achieved a goal, I celebrate. With luck there is never more than a couple of days between celebrations and I sail with a continually renewed feeling of achievement and a sense of going places even if I am in the middle of nowhere. Whatever method of self-motivation you choose I would recommend that it emphasises the positive aspects of events and keeps the negative vibes firmly in their place.

Monitoring Standards

Monitoring someone else's performance and making sure they come up to the mark is easy. Keeping a check on your own performance is hard. When you are short-handed, letting standards slip is easy. Surely the washing up can wait? That sheet was fine when you checked it yesterday and nothing much could have happened to it since. The rigging screws were tight yesterday. How could they be slack today? Surely it is too rough to change the engine oil?

You understand your own shortcomings so well that excuses that you would regard as fatuous from anyone else carry the ring of truth. At first you are well aware that you are accepting second-rate, slipshod work but does it matter if it works? The answer is, 'Yes'. because standards slip across the board and in time you accept second-rate as the norm. Eventually there will be an occasion when only your very best efforts will save the day, and if you have lost the habit you will have problems.

Maintaining standards is easy when the winds and seas are kind and you are well fed and rested. It is much harder when you are tired or suffering from seasickness or scared out of your wits. It is easy to view the Victorian explorers dressing for dinner in the jungle as figures of fun but in their own way they were trying to maintain their personal standards. They used simple social rituals as an easy yardstick to judge if standards were slipping. Every short-handed sailor must find their own way of maintaining their standards, judging their performance and identifying the early warning signs when they are falling below par. Black ties are optional.

Morale

Everyone suffers from good and bad days. In the good times all is easy and the world full of bright, cheerful colours then, for no apparent reason you are sucked into the depths of a black hole from which there is no escape. I do not know what triggers these oscillations or how to avoid or predict them. All I know is they arrive when least expected and after outstaying their welcome, depart.

Giving yourself a treat can help. I have a sweet tooth and squirrel away sweets for this purpose. Music can also cheer me up. At their kindest others describe my musical tastes as 'cosmopolitan' but at sea I can play what I want, as loudly as I want for as long as I want. Finally, rest is a great aid. It is easy to become depressed when you are tired and see no end to your struggles. A good sleep can cheer you up and let you see everything in a different light.

Running through all this is the idea that the single-hander's self reliance comes from a strong sense of self-discipline. I feel a hypocrite saying this for I am one of nature's slobs, naturally untidy and never do anything today that I can postpone until tomorrow. I believe 'manyana' describes unnecessary haste. This will not wash at sea. The weather may have been rubbish for days with forty-knot squalls pounding the boat every few minutes and dragging me from my bunk to tend the sails. Even brewing a coffee has become a challenge. I am tired, cold and all I want to do is to sit under a tree with a beer but I still have to make those boring checks (no, they can't wait), tend to the sails and keep the boat sailing safely. I am driven not from a sense of duty or from some innate inner strength of character but from plain ordinary fear and self-interest. I know that if I do not carry out those checks then something will fail and the minutes I save now by not doing this work will, with interest, be set against the hours it takes making good the mess. I tend the sails to keep the boat moving because my best chance of escaping horrible weather is to sail out of it. I brew coffee and cook meals because I know that I am burning up energy at a tremendous rate and I prefer eating hot food and drinking hot drinks than cold.

Self-discipline is essential to the short-handed sailor. Without it you are doomed to spend your life seeking excuses for failure. Whether it comes from nobility and strength of character or, like mine, springs from base, ignoble self-interest does not matter. You must have it if you wish to make safe, enjoyable passages.

DEBRIEFING

I know of no courses that teach you how to be a short-handed sailor. Perhaps the nearest are the qualifying cruises for short-handed races where, if you survive, you can join in the race. I am not sure of the value of going out with an instructor and pretending to be short-handed. Having a safety net can induce a false sense of confidence.

Perhaps it is best to learn from both your failures and successes but these lessons should only take place after the event, when the adrenaline has stopped flowing, all is quiet and it is possible to take a detached, impersonal viewpoint. There is a far better chance of finding sensible answers when you have calmed down, and are free of the dangers of tunnel vision when all you do is justify your actions. Then you can ask:

- What went well?
- What could have been done better?
- What worked?
- What did not work?
- What were the skills you lacked?
- What equipment did you lack?
- How could the problem been avoided in the first place?

Some of the truths that emerge may be hard to accept, but to ignore them is foolish.

Not all these lessons are learnt at sea. I was in St Martin, in the north-east Caribbean, ready to leave for the Azores the instant what the local radio called 'unseasonable northerlies' were replaced by the Trades. It was the end of April and as the days passed I grew more and more concerned about the approaching hurricane season. I wanted to be close to the Azores before the end of June. If the remnants of a hurricane or tropical storm did appear while I was at sea I needed the maximum amount of warning to get out of its way. Receiving weather forecasts at sea was a priority and I liked the idea of supplementing the US Coastguard's High Seas forecast with weather faxes.

I had a laptop computer. I had been given a shareware weather fax programme. All I needed was a demodulator to translate the radio's analogue signal into a digital signal the computer would understand. There was not a demodulator to be had for love or money on St Martin but I was given a wiring diagram from which I could build my own. There is a Radio Shack in Philipsburg where I could buy all the bits and pieces I needed. Unfortunately circuit boards, diodes, resistors and chips were a mystery, and the wiring diagram could have been in Greek for all it meant to me. I sailed without a weather fax but the next time I crossed the Atlantic I turned making demodulators into a cottage industry to supply those in need.

Short-handed skippering and sailing is not difficult but ultimately its skills can only be learnt at sea and they improve with experience. I admire anyone who has the nerve to buy a boat on Monday and set out across the Atlantic on Tuesday with or without a crew, but I am a prisoner of my prejudices. I learned to sail in dinghies and worked up sailing bigger and bigger boats, sailing farther and farther and acquiring the necessary skills at each stage. I never faced a vertical learning curve.

I learned short-handed sailing the same way. At first passages were short but as expertise and confidence grew and as alterations and modifications made my boat more suitable for sailing alone then passages became longer and more demanding but I was careful never to step too far into the unknown. I had no grand plans and this suited me. Consequently I believe this is the right way to learn to be a short-handed sailor but it takes time. Others with more pressing ambitions have simply stepped aboard and cast off and succeeded. The optimum is probably somewhere between these extremes.

4 Evolutions – Introduction

INTRODUCTION

Many years ago I was invited aboard one of the Ocean Youth Club ketches and for one long weekend between the Solent and Poole everyone aboard found time, whether I was on watch or off, to take me aside and carefully explain that I was not doing things the OYC way. This was not a problem. There are as many ways of changing a sail, reefing, tacking, gybing or coiling a rope as there are yachts and most of them work. This applies to single-handed sailors as well as fully crewed yachts but single-handed sailors have the dilemma of carrying out two actions in different parts of the boat simultaneously. If you have found one particular way that suits you that is fine.

All I can do is describe the problems I have encountered and the solutions that work for me, and may use them as a starting point to find your own answers. For brevity and convenience they are described from the single-hander's point of view. Modified to allow for the assistance of one or two crew members the advice is also useful to the short-handed sailor.

CONCURRENT AND SEQUENTIAL ACTIONS

It is a pity that the speed at which a manoeuvre is executed is taken as a measure of a crew's ability and a vessel's overall efficiency. Attempting to observe this dictum, the single-handed sailor rushes from one task to the next determined to show that he is as good as any fully crewed yacht. In his haste he does nothing particularly well and frequently makes avoidable and embarrassing errors.

Measured by the stopwatch, efficiency requires large crews, with each member responsible for a single action. Individuals are adept at a single skill or even one of its subdivisions with, for example, specialist mainsail trimmers rather than general purpose sail trimmers. It is production line crewing with everyone concerned solely over their small part in a much bigger picture. Speed is achieved by carrying out several actions more or less simultaneously. This is concurrent action.

As the numbers on board diminish, each remaining crew member takes responsibility for more and more tasks until the single-hander finds that he has to do everything by himself and can only perform an evolution by carrying out one action after another. Teamwork is replaced by sequential action.

Consider a manoeuvre as simple as tacking. On a crewed boat the skipper has a role equivalent to an orchestral conductor, a maestro, who ensures that everyone joins in and plays their part at the correct moment. He tells the helmsman when to put the helm a-lee and then brings everyone in on cue. Someone tends the mainsheet, another the weather jib sheet, and somebody else the lee jib sheet. There may well be someone on the foredeck to keep a lookout and another to help the jib come through. More or less simultaneously the helm goes over, one jib sheet is cast off, the other hauled in and the mainsheet trimmed, and without the least break in its stride, the yacht settles down on its new course. With sail changes and reefing more crew members are involved but the principle remains the same.

The short-handed sailor must complete the same actions as a series of clearly separated tasks one after another, and the secret of success is carrying them out in the correct order. For tacking, the sequence of actions

Coming alongside

PREPARATIONS

1. Find clear, quiet water where you can heave-to or lie ahull while you carry out preparations to enter harbour.
2. Rig fenders to port and starboard.
3. Rig warps
(a) port and starboard. Have a spare fender to hand in the cockpit.
(b) outside of everything.
(c) from the bows to the cockpit.
(d) from the stern to the cockpit.
4. They should all be longer than you think you might need.
5. They should be ready to hand but secure in the cockpit so that they cannot fall overboard at an inconvenient moment.

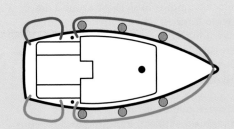

STEPPING ASHORE

1. Jumping ashore is not an option for the short handed sailor..
2. As you come alongside the pontoon (jetty or quay) pick up the bow and stern warps.
3. Move amidships where the gap between your boat and the pontoon is narrowest.
4. Step over guardrails.
5. Step ashore.

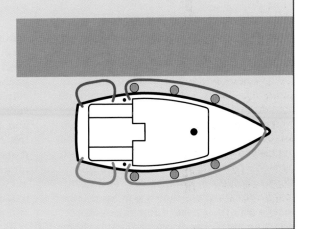

is obvious. Less evident is that throughout the entire evolution he has one hand for the helm and one for each of the sheets in turn. It is possible to tack a boat letting an auto-helm or windvane control the helm but this requires searoom for peace of mind.

While the principle of sequential action applies to every short-handed evolution, a sequence of actions is not a formula applied thoughtlessly. Actions must be modified to take into account conditions, such as sea state, wind, tide, the presence of other boats and you and your crew. If you are tired, each action will take longer and the chances of a making mistake are above average. Make allowances and change your procedures.

It was midnight on my third day at sea and I was trying to anchor off Withersea. I could feel the anchor bouncing along the seabed. It took three attempts to persuade it to stick and I was so tired that the only way I could be sure of not making any stupid mistakes was to sit on my shoulder and tell myself what to do as if I was a retarded novice who could not be trusted to do anything right.

The nearer you are to harbour and your berth, the more evolutions you carry out. Manoeuvres come one after another with little time to catch your breath. As well as planning the sequence of actions for each evolution you must first prepare a shooting script for the entire series of manoeuvres

for there is no time to stop and think
between finishing one and starting the
next. Stress levels are high, for all is taking
place in confined waters. Short-handed
sailors cannot station crew around the
boat to fend off when collision becomes
unavoidable, or make daring leaps ashore
carrying lines. Instead they must achieve
the same result by careful manoeuvring
and cunning.

Offshore manoeuvres are normally
concerned with sail handling and tacking.
Evolutions come singly or, at most, in pairs.
There is plenty of searoom and there is
no pressure of time. Sometimes you think
about tacking for a couple of days before
taking any action.

PLANNING AND PREPARATION

Planning and preparations must be complete
before beginning any manoeuvre. Suddenly
remembering that you need an extra fender,
the boathook or another line is usually the
prelude to chaos. You must be ready for all
contingencies. For example, always have
warps and fenders ready port and starboard
as you go alongside. Fenders should be put
out before warps and warps should be led
outside of everything, including fenders.
Warps should run from the bow and stern
to the cockpit where they are to hand either
to take ashore or pass to someone ashore.
When you tack, check every sheet is running
free before putting the helm over. If you
are working on deck put on your harness
and check the jackstays before leaving the
cockpit.

If possible, always rehearse what you plan
to do. Alone, this may be no more than
running through a mental checklist but if
you have a crew it may be worthwhile
carrying out a dry run.

Carry every manoeuvre out as slowly as
wind and tide permit. This is not saying,
'Go slow.' In strong winds and tides, control
comes from speed, but unnecessarily fast
manoeuvres reduce margins of error and
are upsetting when they go wrong.

If your boat is tiller steered think about
fitting a tiller extension to allow for some
degree of movement around the cockpit
when helming.

KNOW YOUR BOAT

Every skipper, but especially the single-
hander, should know the performance of
their boat under sail and power, and the
only way to learn this is go to sea and play.
How does your boat carry its way in various
conditions of wind and tide? When losing
way or stopped, how quickly do the bows
blow off in various wind strengths? How
does you boat handle astern? Going astern
can you drive the stern through the wind in
a strong breeze? This type of knowledge is
especially important when coming alongside
a wall or a pontoon.

Can you steer your yacht with the sails?
Steering by adjusting the balance of the sails
used to be a standard exercise for aspiring
yachtsmen. The tiller would be lashed amid
ships and thereafter changing the trim of the
sails changed course. It works well beating
and close reaching on long-keeled yachts
but can be difficult on fin and skeg yachts.
A short choppy sea can make it impossible
for any yacht. Given the popularity of
auto-helms and windvanes this sounds
like a pointless exercise until one day the
autohelm or windvane, or both, pack up.

If you let go of the helm how long will your
boat hold its course under sail or under
power? Often when you are entering a
harbour or coming alongside you may have
to leave the helm briefly to consult the chart,
sort out the fenders or free a snagged line,
and it is useful to know how much time you
have before you must dash back to the helm.
How long your boat holds its course will vary
depending on how fast it is going, the wind
and the sea state. Under power you may find
it helps when you leave the helm to knock
the engine out of gear so that there is no
prop wash to disturb the rudder.

How easy is it to stem wind and tide, and
hold a position? This is normally done under
engine and is straightforward when wind

The Paddle Wheel Effect

The effect is important when manouevring at slow speeds.

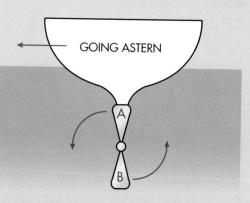

GOING ASTERN

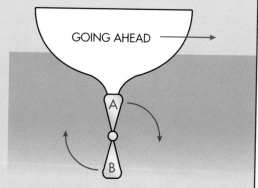

GOING AHEAD

STERN MOVES TO STARBOARD
Effect can be countered by rudder

The effect of the blade at A is to turn the stern to port.
The effect of the blade at B is to turn the stern to
starboard. B is in deeper water than A and has
greater effect with the result stern moves to starboard.

STERN MOVES TO PORT
Effect cannot be countered by rudder

The effect of the blade at A is to turn the stern to port.
The effect of the blade at B is to turn the stern to
starboard. B is in deeper water than A and has
greater effect with the result stern moves to starboard.

The screw race is the stream of water leaving the propeller. It is made up of
(a) the TRANSVERSE COMPONENT which has a sideways effect sometimes
called the PADDLE WHEEL EFFECT
(b) a FORE AND AFT COMPONENT which moves the boat ahead or astern.

When looking from astern a right handed propeller revolves clockwise.
The effect of a left handed propeller is the exact opposite of a right handed propeller.

and tide are together or diametrically opposite each other, when you must first decide whether the wind or the tide is the stronger. You point the bows into the wind (or tide) and adjust the throttle until the boat is stationary relative to a fixed feature. Usually you find that your boat is either creeping slowly ahead or falling slightly back so it is necessary to continuously juggle the throttle.

Holding position is difficult when wind and tide are at an angle to each other. The wind pushes the topsides one way and the tide grips the keel, shoving it in some other direction with the result that the boat lies at

an angle to both wind and tide. Wind over tide can be a useful technique when trying to enter a confined berth. You stem either the wind or the tide and let the other drive the boat in the direction you wish to go. Done well, you can have your boat travelling sideways and it is sometimes used to come alongside another boat or a pontoon.

How quickly does your boat stop at various speeds when the engine is put astern? This depends on a combination of how hard you go astern, how fast you are going in the first place and what the wind and tide are doing. The safe way to discover the answer is to find a buoy in open water and approach the

buoy from various angles, aiming to stop with the buoy close abeam.

What is your boat's turning circle at various speeds to port and to starboard? Depending on whether you have a right- or left-handed propeller your turning circle to port (or starboard) will be greater. This is because the propeller acts like a paddle wheel and pushes the stern round.

The faster you are travelling the harder you can put the helm over and the tighter your boat's turning circle. At slow speeds, putting the helm hard over turns the rudder into a brake and stops the boat. Under power, the exception to this rule is when you put the helm hard over and put the throttle to full ahead for an instant. This throws a wall of water against the rudder, which shoves the stern round and starts the boat swinging. Taking the power off quickly prevents any significant forward motion developing. Repeated two or three times this manoeuvre

can turn a boat through 90 degrees in its own length. It does not work astern.

How does your boat manoeuvre astern? Long-keeled boats are shy about going backwards. When I put *Margo* astern it does not matter where I point the tiller. I never know whether the stern will swing to port or starboard. How soon the rudder responds depends on how long it is before water starts passing across the rudder. Until then the paddle wheel effect of the propeller, wind and tide determines which way the stern will swing. Lightweight yachts will reach steerage way faster than heavy displacement boats. Yachts with outboard engines are at an advantage, for the engine can be used as a stern drive and angled to provide steerage from the start of the evolution.

How does your vessel heave-to? Some boats do, some do not. If your boat does then it is a useful way to stop while you wait for the tide, sort out a problem or just have a cup of tea.

How does your boat lie a-hull? I once believed that there was something more to lying a-hull than taking the sails off, putting the helm down and leaving the boat to look after itself. There is not. Your vessel's windage and hull form will determine the angle you lie at to wind and seas. Lying a-hull is primarily a heavy weather tactic.

With the judicious use of a fender or a warp, an alert crew can conceal their skipper's ignorance of his boat's performance from pontoon critics. If the single-handed sailor does not know how his boat handles then his errors are obvious to all. Rather than learning from your mistakes, practice these manoeuvres in clear water and varying conditions whenever the opportunity arises.

Confidence in the knowledge of how your boat performs is important when others advise on how to perform an evolution. It is surprising how many people feel free to offer advice on how to carry out a manoeuvre. It may be a harbourmaster instructing you to berth in an impossible position or other skippers being helpful. The essence of their advice are variations on the theme that you can make your boat do the impossible regardless of the risk of damaging your boat or someone else's. If you question their recommendations they loudly inform the gathering crowd that any landlubber could carry out the manoeuvre with their eyes closed and arms folded. Stand your ground. Firstly, you know your boat and they do not. Secondly, their judgement automatically includes a crew of thousands hauling on lines and fending off while you must use the wind, tide and helm to achieve the same result. Nearly always this takes longer and requires more searoom than they can imagine.

But do not ignore other yachtsmen. If you intend to carry out an evolution that involves any other craft it is good practice to contact their skippers in good time, tell them of your intentions and how you plan to carry them out. As a rule they will be pleased to help.

5 Evolutions – Casting Off

When you leave a harbour or anchorage you have the enormous advantage that you start your manoeuvres at a time and place of your choosing. Before you begin there is always time to look around, plan what you are going to do, and if you think it necessary, enlist some help. Everything is in your favour although it helps when casting off, or going alongside, to:

- keep the boathook and a spare fender and line to hand in the cockpit;
- check all warps and lines run free;
- ask for assistance from those on shore;
- complete an evolution in stages e.g. if casting off, facing the wrong way and space is limited, then warp round, berth again, sort out lines and fenders and then cast off.

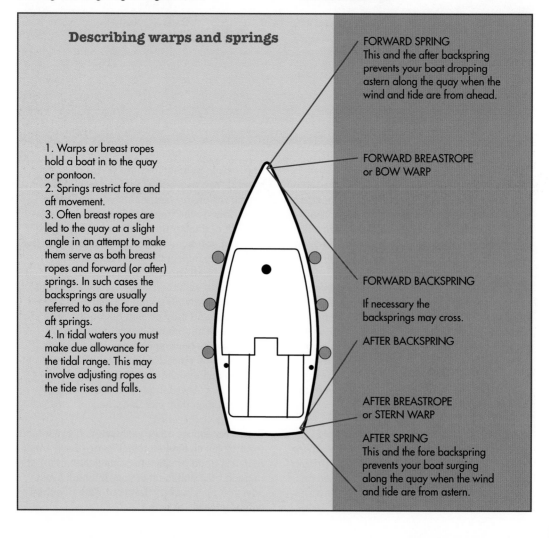

Describing warps and springs

1. Warps or breast ropes hold a boat in to the quay or pontoon.
2. Springs restrict fore and aft movement.
3. Often breast ropes are led to the quay at a slight angle in an attempt to make them serve as both breast ropes and forward (or after) springs. In such cases the backsprings are usually referred to as the fore and aft springs.
4. In tidal waters you must make due allowance for the tidal range. This may involve adjusting ropes as the tide rises and falls.

FORWARD SPRING
This and the after backspring prevents your boat dropping astern along the quay when the wind and tide are from ahead.

FORWARD BREASTROPE or BOW WARP

FORWARD BACKSPRING

If necessary the backsprings may cross.

AFTER BACKSPRING

AFTER BREASTROPE or STERN WARP

AFTER SPRING
This and the fore backspring prevents your boat surging along the quay when the wind and tide are from astern.

Leaving pontoon ahead with favourable wind and tide

TIDE

WIND

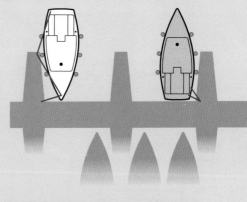

STEP ONE
1. Start engine.
2. Take off all lines except a doubled stern warp.
3. When ready slip and allow wind and tide to carry the boat forward out of the berth.

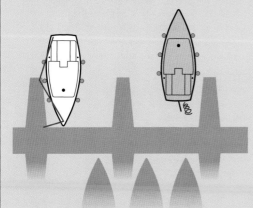

STEP TWO
1. As you begin to clear the finger pontoon and any nearby boats put the helm over.
2. Give the engine a short burst ahead to start the bow swinging put put in neutral before picking up way. How quickly your boat swings round depends on its underwater profile.

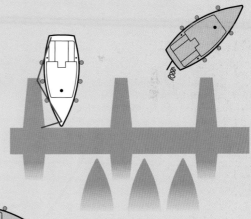

STEP THREE
1. Give further short bursts ahead as necessary to keep the bows swinging round.
2. If you pick up way then try going astern but pause for a second in neutral before putting the engine astern.
3. Some boats using this technique can turn in their own length but allow a couple of boat lengths to be safe.

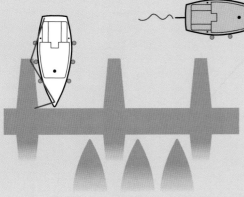

STEP FOUR
1. Once the bows are pointing in the right direction motor out of the marina.

Leaving pontoon ahead with contrary wind and tide

WIND   TIDE

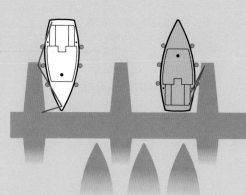

STEP ONE
1. Start engine.
2. Remove all lines except one spring. This will hold the stern off the pontoon and should be ready to slip.
3. When ready put engine ahead and begin to drive out of berth.

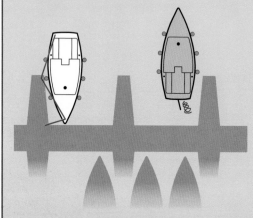

STEP TWO
1. As boat moves forward slip spring. Best to do this with the engine in neutral in case the line falls in the water.
2. With line safely inboard put rudder over and give the engine a short burst ahead to start the bows swinging.

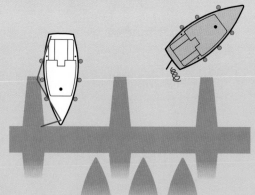

STEP THREE
1. The wind should blow the bows round pretty smartly but another burst or two ahead may be necessary to keep the bows swinging round.
2. Be careful that the wind and tide do not carry you down onto the finger pontoon or other boats. Give them a wide berth.

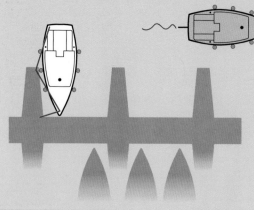

STEP FOUR
1. When the bows are pointing in the right direction drive out of the marina.

Leaving pontoon ahead with cross wind and tide

STEP ONE

1. With the wind blowing and tide streaming across the finger pontoons there is the real danger of being carried onto the finger pontoon opposite or onto other boats before you have enough way to have control.

2. If your boat is small enough it may be better to take the lines off stand on the finger pontoon and feed your boat out of its berth hand over hand

3. If your boat is too big or the wind and tide too strong consider enlisting some volunteers from nearby boats.

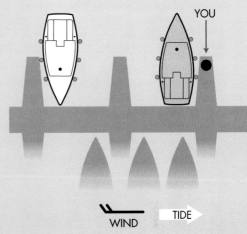

YOU

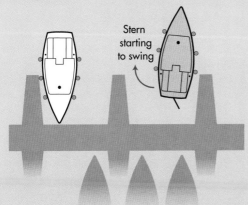

Stern starting to swing

WIND   TIDE

STEP TWO

1. As the stern of your boat approaches the end of the finger pontoon give the stern a shove to start the bows swinging round and step aboard.

STEP THREE

1. Once aboard put the helm over and feed the engine bursts of power to keep the bows swinging round.

2. With wind and tide against you then you might need some forward way to avoid dropping back onto other boats.

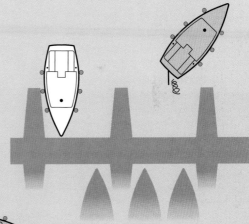

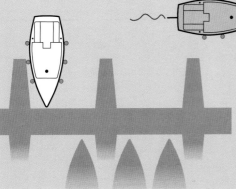

STEP FOUR

1. Once pointing in the right direction drive out of the marina.

The technique is much the same if the wind and tide are carrying onto the finger pontoon except if you simply drive out you may bump along the finger pontoon. Consider handing your boat out as before. Once clear of the finger pontoon the wind and tide should swing the bows round pretty quickly.

Leaving pontoon astern with favourable wind and tide

STEP ONE

1. Start engine
2. Remove all lines except for a doubled stern line.
3. Put the rudder over.
4. Put the engine astern.
5. Wait a second or two then slip. Your boat will not start to swing in your chosen direction until water is passing across the rudder and you have steerage way. How quickly your boat swings round depends on its underwater profile. At slow speeds the paddle wheel effect of the prop can be significant.

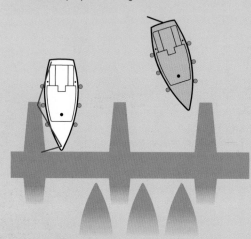

STEP TWO

1. The aim is to have the bows swinging round as you clear the finger pontoon and any nearby boats.
2. The wind and tide should help the bows round but it is a good idea to go astern as far as possible and give yourself as much room as possible before starting Step 3.

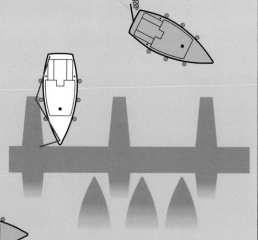

STEP THREE

1. Once well clear of the pontoon put the rudder over and give a burst ahead to keep the bows coming round.
2. Depending on the space available you may need to go astern to take the way off while the bows conrinue to swing.
3. As you gain forward way remember that although the bows continue to swing the wind and tide will be carrying you towards other boats. Keep a sharp all round look out.

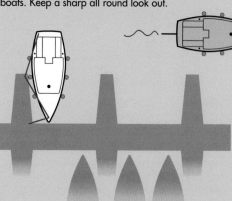

STEP FOUR

1. Once the bows are pointing in the right direction heave a sigh of relief and drive out of the marina.

WIND　　　　TIDE

Leaving pontoon astern with contrary or cross wind and tide

If you are lying bows to the pontoon and the wind is contrary or blowing onto the finger pontoon or other boats then you should consider enlisting some help.

STEP ONE
1. Enlist help.
2. Start engine.
3. Remove lines.
4. Begin moving boat out of berth, using engine to assist if necessary.

STEP TWO
1. Still using the engine as necessary the boat is moved aft while being kept clear of the finger pontoon.

STEP THREE
1. As the bows clear the finger pontoon they are swung around.

STEP FOUR
1. Using the boathook and a gentle prod ahead of the engine helps bring the bows around.

STEP FIVE
1. A mixture of hands and boathook keeps the boat clear of other parked boats.
2. With the bows pointing in the right direction drive out of the marina.

LEAVING FINGER PONTOONS

As a rule leaving a marina finger pontoon is straightforward. Problems begin when the marina operator has squeezed in more berths by making the gaps between the lines of pontoons very narrow. How narrow may not be apparent when you sail in but backing out can be a challenge, particularly in strong winds. Steerageway astern varies from vessel to vessel but it will be non-existent until some speed has built up. This takes distance and you may not have enough. Frequently you must leave the berth and start turning the bows in the direction you wish to sail without steerage way. In practice this means standing on the pontoon, pushing your boat astern, stepping aboard at the last minute, keeping clear of the boats on either side and possibly relying on the judicious use of a boathook on their guardrails, pushpit and pulpit to speed you on your way. Once clear with the bows swinging in the direction you wish to go, head for the cockpit and take over the helm.

LEAVING A BOX

A box is the Dutch and German term for a marina berth and often you lie to a pontoon with lines out to piles. You are normally bows to the pontoon. When you come to leave, the first task is have all lines ready to slip, then check every line again ...carefully. A line jamming can ruin everything just as you begin to relax. Start the engine, cast off the bow lines and head for the cockpit. Once there, pull on both stern lines to get your vessel underway. Once your boat begins moving astern flick stern lines off the piles and return towards the bows pushing on whichever pile that will start the stern swinging in the direction you want the bows to point.

In practice you stay abeam the pile and walk forwards along the side deck as the boat slips aft. When the bows begin to clear the piles, and still standing in the bows, give a final shove with the boathook on the pile to complete the turn. All that remains is to return to the cockpit and drive out the marina. It may not be elegant but it works. The greatest risk is probably your bows

Springing Off.

swinging round too early and catching the boat alongside, but by moving forward towards the bows as you leave the box you are in a good position to fend off other boats and this threat is much reduced. If, for some reason, you have backed into a box then your departure will be much easier. The procedure is much the same as for backing out except that once you have slipped the bow lines you remain the cockpit throughout, for the danger now is that the stern will catch one of the boats alongside especially if you yield to temptation and start your turn too early.

Never assume that there is no tidal current in a marina. Sometimes it can run quite hard, and the basic procedure outlined above will vary depending upon the wind and tide.

SPRINGING OFF

Springing off describes using a combination of a warp and engine power to swing the bows or the stern away from a pontoon or quay wall. It is used when space is restricted and you cannot simply drive out ahead. If you have to spring off a pontoon or a wall then make sure that the springs are doubled and led back to cockpit where they can be

Leaving box ahead with favourable wind and tide

STEP ONE
1. Start engine.
2. Slip all but stern lines.
3. When ready slip stern lines.
4. Put engine slow ahead and
drive out box.

Some boxes have lines strung between
the piles and the pontoons. These are
good for hauling your boat in and out.
Have boathook ready to grab them.

Some boxes have short finger
pontoons. This can help going ashore
when backing in and physically
separates boats.

WIND

TIDE

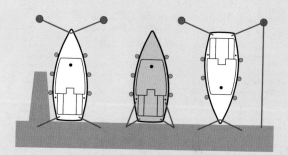

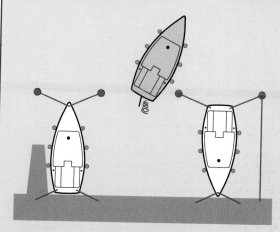

STEP TWO
1. As you clear the piles put rudder
over.
2. Give short burst ahead to start
bows swinging. Some boxes are
very tight and you may need to
completely clear the piles before
beginning your swing. If space
ahead is restricted then go very
slowly as you clear the piles to keep
forward speed down as you swing.

STEP THREE
1. Once clear of the box and
pointing in the right direction
motor out of marina.

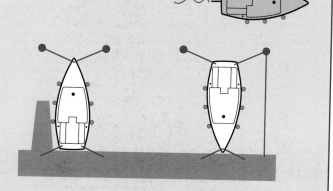

Leaving box ahead with contrary wind and tide

STEP ONE
1. Start engine.
1. When ready, start engine.
2. Slip all warps but bow warps.
3. Put engine ahead.
4. Slip bow warps and drive out of box. To avoid dropping back onto the pontoon it may help to be going slow ahead as you slip the bow warps and/or arrange for the bow warps to be slipped from the cockpit.

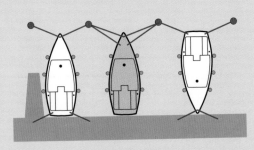

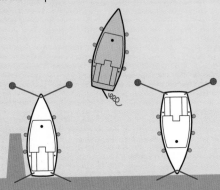

STEP TWO
1. As you clear the piles put the helm over and give the engine a burst ahead.
2. If the berth is tight then you may need to be completely clear of the piles before beginning to swing.

STEP THREE
1. The wind should blow the bows round pretty smartly but additional bursts ahead may be necessary to keep the bows swinging.
2. Be careful that the wind and tide do not push you down onto other boats.

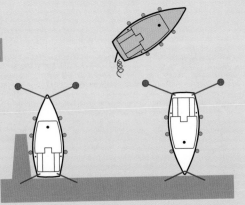

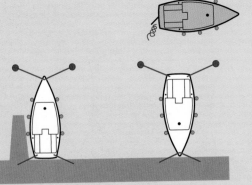

TIDE

WIND

STEP FOUR
1. When pointing in the right direction motor out of the marina.

Leaving box ahead with cross wind and tide

STEP ONE
1. Start engine.
2. Remove all lines except those on the upwind/uptide side.
3. If the wind/tide will turn the bows in the direction you wish to go as you clear the box simply putting the helm over and giving a burst ahead should bring the bows round as you clear the box.
4. If not, rig a spring. Whatever the wind/tide is doing shortening this spring will pull you forward in the box.

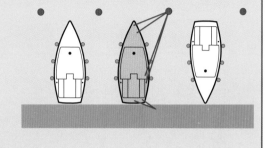

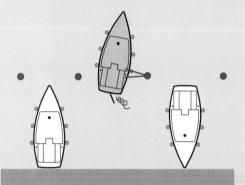

STEP TWO
1. Put engine ahead.
2. Slip bow line.
3. Slip stern line. You should begin to move out of the box. Take in spring to keep it out of the water. You do not want it round the prop.
4. As you clear the box put helm over. You should begin to swing round pile.

STEP THREE
1. As you swing round pile you may need to pay out line to lengthen the spring and keep clear of other boats.
2. The more power you give the engine, the faster you will swing.
3. Always keep tension on spring.

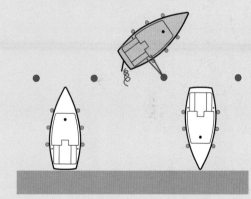

WIND   TIDE

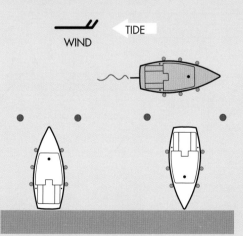

STEP FOUR
1. As you come onto course, stop swing.
2. Put engine in neutral.
3. Slip spring.
4. Drive out of marina.

This technique is useful when turning space is limited and when going out astern. Even though you will not have steerage way until water is passing across the rudder the spring will pull you round. The greatest problem usually is backing off the pontoon and getting far enough out of the box to start the turn.

Leaving box astern

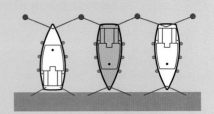

STEP ONE
1. Start engine.
2. Make all lines ready to slip.

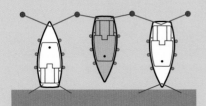

STEP TWO
1. Slip bow lines.
2. Depending on wind and tide it is likely that the bows will blow off pretty quickly. Hurry back to cockpit.

STEP THREE
1. Haul on lines to start boat moving aft out of the box.
2. When boat is moving slip lines.
3. Check all lines are in boat and none are trailing in the water.

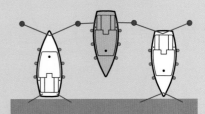

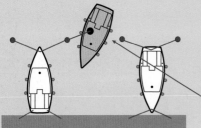

STEP FOUR
1. Stand midships and fend off pile with boathook.
2. This will swing the boat round as it leaves the box.

But watch what is happening here

STEP FIVE
1. As the bows clear the box use the boathook to keep the bows swinging round.
2. When bows are pointing in direction of travel go to the cockpit.

But still watch what is happening here

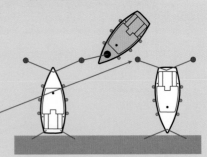

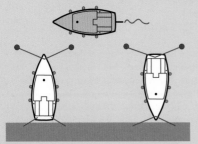

STEP SIX
1. Motor into clear water and stow warps and fenders.
2. Proceed to sea.

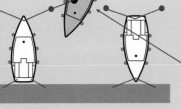

Springing off with wind and tide astern

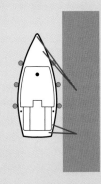

STEP ONE
1. Start engine.
2. Have a couple of spare fenders to hand in the cockpit.
3. Remove all lines except the forward backspring and the stern warp.
4. Put these on slip.

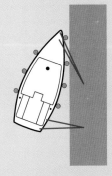

STEP TWO
1. Pay out the stern warp.
2. Under the influence of the wind and tide the forward backspring will tighten up and the stern will spring out.
3. An extra fender may be needed forward.
4. At this stage all is under control and if necessary you can shorten the stern warp and come back into quay.

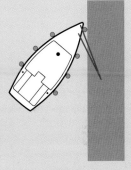

STEP THREE
1. Slip the stern warp.
2. The stern will now swing even further round.

STEP FOUR
1. Let the stern come well out.
2. Put the engine slow astern.
3. Slip the forward backspring.
4. Put the rudder over.
5. Increase revs so as to pull away from the quay and begin to straighten up.

WIND

TIDE

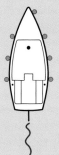

STEP FIVE
1. When pointing in the right direction motor into clear water and tidy away lines and fenders.

Springing off with wind and tide ahead

STEP ONE
1. Start engine.
2. Have a couple of spare fenders to hand in cockpit.
3. Remove all lines except bow warp and aft backspring.
4. Put these on slip.

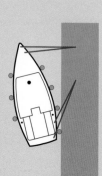

STEP TWO
1. Pay out the stern warp.
1. Pay out bow warp.
2. The wind and tide should start the bows swinging away from the quay.
3. Extra fenders may be needed to protect the stern.
4. At this stage everything is under control. You can always haul in on the bow warp, bring the boat back into the quay and start again.

STEP THREE
1. Slip the bow warp.
2. The bows will continue to swing out.

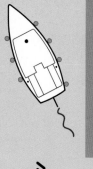

STEP FOUR
1. When bows are well clear of the quay, put the engine slow ahead.
2. Slip the aft backspring.
3. Increase engine revs and drive away from the quay.

WIND

STEP FIVE
1. When clear of quay, straighten up, drive into clear water and tidy away warps and fenders.

TIDE

Springing off with cross wind and tide (1)

STEP ONE
1. The wind but not the tide will blow you off a quay wall BUT the tide
can run under pontoons. If you are lying to a pontoon it is best to
check.
2. Start engine.
3. Have a couple of spare fenders to hand in cockpit.
4. Remove all lines except bow warp and aft backspring.
5. Put these on slip.

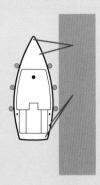

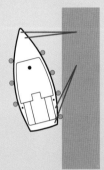

STEP TWO
1. Pay out bow warp.
2. The wind should start the bows swinging away from the quay. If not,
then put the engine astern and increase revs until the bow begins to
swing out.
3. Extra fenders may be needed to protect the stern.
4. At this stage everything is under control. You can always stop the
engine, haul in on the bow warp, bring the boat back into the quay and
start again.

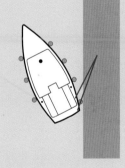

STEP THREE
1. Slip the bow warp.
2. The bows will continue to swing out.

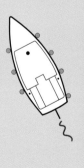

STEP FOUR
1. When bows are well clear of the quay, put
the engine slow ahead.
2. Slip the aft backspring.
3. Increase engine revs and drive away from
the quay.

WIND

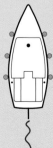

TIDE

STEP FIVE
1. When clear of quay, straighten up,
drive into clear water and tidy away
warps and fenders.

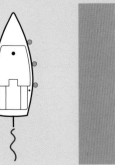

Springing off with cross wind and tide (2)

STEP ONE
1. The wind is blowing you onto a quay wall or pontoon BUT the tide can be running in some other direction. It is best to check.
2. Start engine.
3. Have a couple of spare fenders to hand in cockpit.
4. Remove all lines except bow warp and aft backspring.
5. Put these on slip.

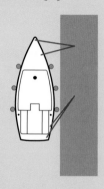

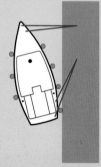

STEP TWO
1. Put the engine astern. Remember without water passing across the rudder you have no steerage way.
2. Pay out bow warp.
3. The bows should begin swinging away from the quay. If not, increase revs until the bow begins to swing out.
4. Extra fenders may be needed to protect the stern.
5. At this stage everything is under control. You can always stop the engine, haul in on the bow warp, bring the boat back into the quay and start again.

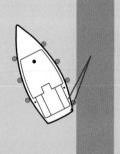

STEP THREE
1. Slip the bow warp.
2. The bows will continue to swing out.

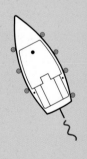

STEP FOUR
1. When bows are well clear of the quay, put the engine slow ahead. Remember to pause for a second in neutral before putting the engine ahead.
2. Slip the aft backspring.
3. Increase engine revs and drive away from the quay.

WIND

TIDE (?)

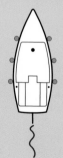

STEP FIVE
1. When clear of quay, straighten up, drive into clear water and tidy away warps and fenders.

Springing off with cross wind and tide (3)

WIND   TIDE

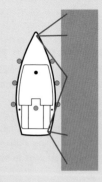

STEP ONE
1. Have extra fenders to hand in cockpit.
2. Start engine.

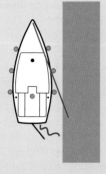

STEP TWO
1. Remove all lines except for one forward backspring which is led well aft. This should be doubled so it can be slipped.
2. Put rudder to starboard.
3. Put engine ahead.

STEP THREE
1. The stern should begin to swing out.
2. If the wind and tide are too strong then unless you can rig a line to a buoy or pile to haul the stern out you must rig a spring and motor ahead to bring out the stern.

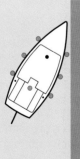

STEP FOUR
1. When the stern is well out slip the spring.
2. Put engine astern and pull bows clear of the pontoon.

STEP FIVE
1. Straighten up, motor to clear water and tidy away warps and fenders.
2. Proceed to sea.

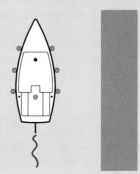

cast off without you leaving the helm. One end of the spring should be just long enough to reach the cockpit. When the time comes to slip, this is the end you loosen off and pull in to reduce the chance of wrapping a line round your prop.

LEAVING A RAFT OF BOATS

Unless you are the outside boat, sailing off a raft of boats can be a nightmare. It will nearly always require the assistance of others. This should be arranged well in advance and everyone must be fully aware of your intentions and the role they are to play. This may require some negotiation.

If you are the outside boat but one it is usual for the outside boat to take off their bow shore line and put lines onto the boat inside you with their bow line going round your stern outside of everything. Their bow then blows, or is pushed, off, opening a gap for you to sail through. You slip your lines and drive out while the crew of the outside boat pull on their lines until they lie nicely alongside.

If you are buried deep inside a raft with rafts of boats ahead and astern it is impossible to drive out, and to add to your problems, there will be a huge tangle of shorelines between you and open water. The procedure for freeing yourself from the boat immediately outside you is exactly the same as before and the difficulty he faces of hauling in himself and all the other boats outside him once you are free is his, not yours. Your problem is the huge number of shore lines between you and open water and the fact that the lack of space between your boat and those in the raft ahead probably makes warping out the only sensible solution.

Warping out is a hangover from the days when engineless square riggers moved around harbours and other confined spaces and gives nautical respectability to moving your boat about the harbour by hauling on lines taken ashore or to other boats. Lines at angles to the stern or bow permit manoeuvres to be carried out in a controlled fashion; which would be impossible under power.

The technique is simple. A line is led to the shore (or another boat) in the direction you wish to travel and made fast. Hauling on this line takes you where you wish to go. Paying out a stern line made fast to your starting point controls your rate of advance and allows you to stop at any time.

If you double all your lines so they can slipped and take enormous care in your preparations it is just possible to warp out single-handed but if you are using this technique to leave a raft of boats you cannot manage alone. Shorelines of other boats must be taken off and then made fast again once you are out for boats which have dropped their shorelines to let you out will be swinging to and fro, perhaps threatening others unless there are people around to haul on lines and fend off. This is usually done by those ashore. For you to do this once you are clear of the raft would be extremely difficult and impossible when you are on your own boat heaving on lines. If you are concerned about troubling others you can salve your conscience with the thought that during your stay on the raft you helped others to leave.

Once you are clear of the pontoon, box or raft and in open but still protected calm water, stow all lines and fenders before proceeding to sea.

LEAVING A BUOY

Moored to a single buoy on a swinging mooring you lie bows-to a combination of wind and tide. Your first action is to replace the mooring line with a slip. It helps if you can lead this back to the cockpit via the bow roller. If you intend to sail off the mooring then raise your sails, and as a precaution, start your engine. By backing or filling the jib and/or the main you can swing the bows round so that you will sail off the mooring on your desired tack. When you are happy, slip the mooring line and sail off. If you have been lying to the tide it is likely that initially your leeway will be huge and if there are other boats nearby you may sweep down onto them. If this is the case then using the engine discreetly may save the day.

Leaving raft of boats

STEP ONE

1. With its warps, springs and shore lines every raft is a cat's cradle of rope. If you are an inside boat then some assistance is required to find a way through this maze.

2. Your first task is to arrange for the crews from the boats on either side to be present when you sail.

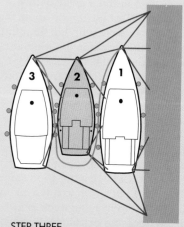

STEP TWO

1. A line from the bows of boat 3 is led outside of everything round the stern of boat 2 and made fast to the bows of boat 1.

2. Another line is led from the stern of boat 3 to the stern of boat 1.

3. Start your engine.

STEP THREE

1. Boat 2 removes all its lines, including shore lines.

2. Boat 3 removes all its lines except
(a) its stern shoreline
(b) the lines it rigged in step one

3. Boat 3 normally begins to swing out giving boat 2 enough space to begin motoring slowly out. Watch out for fenders becoming entangled.

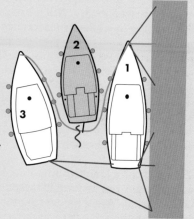

NOTE
This basic procedure will vary slightly to take wind and tide into account.

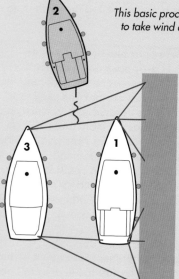

STEP FOUR

1. As boat 2 motors clear, hauling on the lines rigged in step one pulls boat 3 up against boat 1.

2. In heavy winds or if there are a number of boats outside of boat 3 this may require the lines being led to a winch.

3. Meanwhile boat 2 finds clear water and stows its fenders and lines before heading to sea.

If you are lying between two buoys it is usual to drop the stern mooring and then sail off the mooring as though you are lying to a single buoy. Difficulties begin when you are part of a long trot of boats and the wind and tide are carrying you down onto the boats ahead. The bow mooring must be dropped first. Attempts to sail off may carry you onto other boats before you have picked up enough speed to steer clear and there may be no alternative but to motor off the mooring. If the engine is used then great care should be taken to ensure the bridle between the buoys is kept clear of the propeller.

LEAVING AN ANCHORAGE

If you are lying to more than one anchor then raise all but the bower anchor. Stow these anchors and their rodes. You will now be lying to wind and tide and you can begin hauling up the bower anchor. The moment of truth comes when the anchor is up and down and the question is, 'Will it break out?' A tripping line offers reassurance but if the anchorage is busy then the buoy of the tripping line skittering around when you are at anchor is a nuisance to other boats, and if you do need to trip the anchor, there is every chance it will be out of your reach unless you sail up to it. Then you have the problem of catching hold of the buoy before it blows out of reach.

Far better to use a long tripping line, bring it back onboard and tie it off to the pulpit when anchoring. When recovering the anchor the tripping line is brought in with the anchor rode and should the anchor fail to break out all it takes is a strong pull on the tripping line and you carry on hauling both lines aboard. If you do use a tripping line then allow more time for tidying away the anchor chain. In the water the tripping line hardly ever twists round the anchor chain but as chain and line heap together on the foredeck they form a tangle that must be separated before they can be stowed.

If the anchor's reluctance to break out is because has just dug in deep and you have no tripping line, then, having taken in all the rode that you can, driving up to the anchor and giving a burst of power will normally break it out. Sailing an anchor out works well on crewed yachts but for the single-hander life becomes complicated. First, when the anchor is free do you work on the foredeck with the headsail banging round your ears or do you take time to roll it away before going forward? What do you do about the mainsail? Do you leave it up but flogging hoping that it will not catch the wind and take you on a tour of the anchorage? Will the boom slopping to and fro interfere as you travel between the bows and the cockpit? There are no set answers. Each case must be decided on its merits.

On a couple of occasions I have failed to fit a tripping line and the anchor snagged as I retrieved it. Once, having tried sailing the anchor out, I put a rolling hitch on the anchor rode and took a line back to a sheet winch in the hope the extra power would break the anchor out. It pulled the bows down. Reluctantly, the water was cold, I put on a mask and fins and hauled myself down the anchor rode carrying a line with a snaplink on its end. The anchor had snagged a cable. With the snap link clipped into the anchor's crown I had a tripping line. Back on board I lowered the anchor back to the seabed and pulled the anchor up on the tripping line.

Once the anchor has broken out the problem is dropping down on nearby yachts in the time between breaking the anchor out of the ground and getting it aboard. It does not matter if you are using muscle power or a winch, there will be several moments when your boat will be adrift and not under command. If you have a crew then one person could be on the helm and the engine fired up so that they can manoeuvre clear of other vessels while the anchor is brought aboard.

Once the anchor has broken out, controlled speed is of the essence and you may have to temporarily secure the anchor to keep whatever chain you have brought aboard,

Sailing off a buoy with wind rode

Wind and tide in the same direction is sometimes referred to as a LEE-TIDE. When wind and tide are opposed it is called a WEATHER-TIDE.

WIND   TIDE

STEP ONE
1. Rig a doubled line between the buoy and the bows.
2. Let it take the weight.
3. Remove the original mooring line.
4. Hoist the mainsail and leave the mainsheet slightly loose.

STEP TWO
1. Put the helm over. The tide passing across the rudder provides steerage way.
2. The boat will sheer far enough to one side to let the mainsail draw.
3. Ease the mainsheet and go forward.

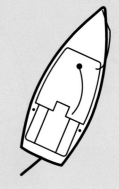

STEP THREE
1. Slip the mooring line.
2. Return to the cockpit.
3. Sheet in mainsail. You will now be sailing close hauled.
4. Unroll (or raise) jib.
5. Sheet in and proceed to sea.

Sailing off a buoy with weather tide

STEP ONE
1. The wind direction will make it difficult to hoist the main until you are underway.
2. Replace the mooring line with a doubled line ready to slip.
3. Unroll (or hoist) the jib.
4. Go forward, slip the mooring line and return to the cockpit.

When the tide is stronger than the wind a vessel is TIDE RODE. When the wind is stronger than the tide a vessel is WIND RODE.

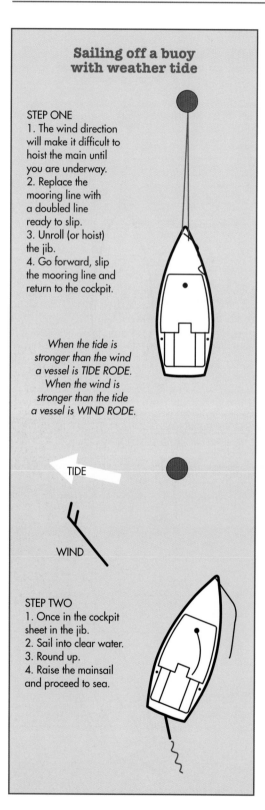

TIDE

WIND

STEP TWO
1. Once in the cockpit sheet in the jib.
2. Sail into clear water.
3. Round up.
4. Raise the mainsail and proceed to sea.

Getting underway moored to buoys fore and aft

STEP ONE
1. Start engine.

STEP TWO
1. Replace both fore and aft mooring ropes with slip ropes.

STEP THREE
1. If the weight is being taken by the bow slip rope then slip the stern line and lie to the bow slip rope.
2. If the weight is being taken by the stern slip rope then slip the bow line and lie top the stern slip rope.
3. If the tide is giving steerage way across the rudder then it may be possible to put the rudder over and steer the boat in the direction you wish to sail off.

STEP FOUR
1. Slip the bow (or the stern) line.
2. Put the engine ahead.
3. Proceed to sea.

CAUTIONS
1. Often the mooring buoys are small enough to be brought aboard and you lie to their mooring line. If so,
(a) there is no need to rig slip ropes. You simply cast off.
(b) there is usually a briddle, just below the water's surface, linking the two buoys and great care must be exercised not to suck this into the prop when you put the engine ahead.

2. The sequence of events is followed when lying between two piles.

Sailing off a single buoy in a lee tide and in restricted waters

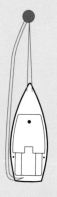

STEP ONE
1. Sometimes there is no room to sail off ahead after you slip the buoy. There may not even be room to turn under engines.
2. Replace the bow line with a slip rope.
3. At the same time rig a slip rope from the buoy outside everything to the stern.

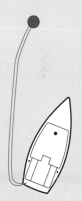

STEP TWO
1. Start the boat sheering to one side by putting the rudder over. The tide passing across the rudder gives steerage way.
2. Slip the bow rope.
3. Let the boat continue to swing round on the tide until the stern line takes the weight.

STEP THREE
1. Unroll (or hoist) the jib.
2. Leave it loosely sheeted.
3. Slip the stern line.

WIND

TIDE

STEP FOUR
1. Sheet in the jib.
2. Sail into waters where there is space to round up and hoist the mainsail.
3. Proceed to sea.

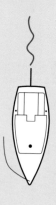

Sailing off an anchor in no tide or lee tide

STEP ONE
1. Before starting always look around and check the position of any other craft in the anchor.
2. Check what they are doing. If a nearby boat is getting underway it is probably best to wait until it is clear. If another boat is entering the anchorage make sure it will be well clear of you.
3. Hoist the mainsail. Leave the sheet loose.
4. Go forward to the anchor.

STEP TWO
1. Pull in the chain until the anchor is up and down.
2. If the anchor breaks out easily then haul in the rest of the chain as quickly as possible.
3. If the anchor does not break out easily then either
(a) start the engine and drive it out.
(b) pay out the chain, or most of it, and sheer from side to side 'tacking' up towards the anchor. Hopefully you will eventually sail beyond (ie 'over') the anchor and pull it out.
4. With the anchor free, it is a fraught time for the short-handed sailor, for once the anchor is broken out you are at the mercy of the wind and the tide with the risk of being carried down onto nearby boats. In a busy anchorage it is probably safer to forget sailing off the anchor and start engine. Even so in strong winds and tides it may be necessary to make the chain fast, dash to the cockpit and motor clear of other boats before returning to the bows. Motoring with the chain hanging from the bows has the real risk of picking up another boat's chain. This will not endear you to its skipper.

STEP THREE
1. It is rare for chain to slide quickly down a hawse pipe. You will probably end up with the anchor on top of a heap of chain on the foredeck.
2. Once the anchor is aboard return to the cockpit.
3. Sheet in the main.
4. Sail into clear waters where you can tidy away the anchor and its chain.
5. Proceed to sea.

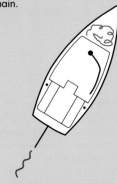

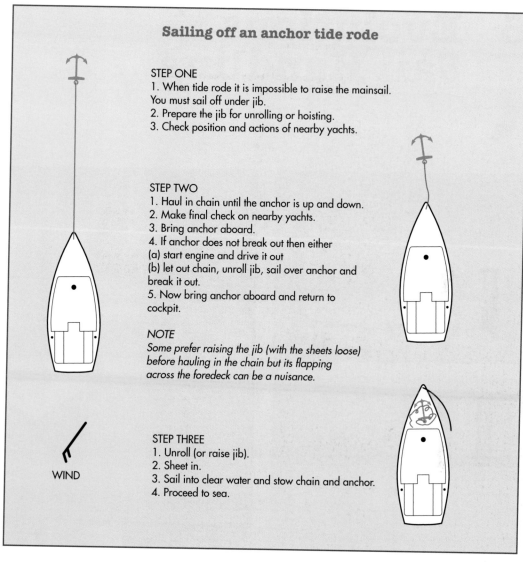

Sailing off an anchor tide rode

STEP ONE
1. When tide rode it is impossible to raise the mainsail. You must sail off under jib.
2. Prepare the jib for unrolling or hoisting.
3. Check position and actions of nearby yachts.

STEP TWO
1. Haul in chain until the anchor is up and down.
2. Make final check on nearby yachts.
3. Bring anchor aboard.
4. If anchor does not break out then either
(a) start engine and drive it out
(b) let out chain, unroll jib, sail over anchor and break it out.
5. Now bring anchor aboard and return to cockpit.

NOTE
Some prefer raising the jib (with the sheets loose) before hauling in the chain but its flapping across the foredeck can be a nuisance.

STEP THREE
1. Unroll (or raise jib).
2. Sheet in.
3. Sail into clear water and stow chain and anchor.
4. Proceed to sea.

WIND

dash to the cockpit and steer clear of other boats. Manoeuvring with the anchor dangling deep in the water is fraught with danger. Unless you are very careful there is a real danger of snagging another anchor line. This will not make you popular.

In busy anchorages it may be necessary to leave the anchor and chain in a heap on the foredeck while you sail clear of other boats particularly if, as on so many boats, the anchor chain is reluctant to slide down the hawse. Once in clear water but still in the protection of the anchorage the chain and

anchor can be securely stowed before heading out to sea.

If your anchor chain has to be fed down the hawse pipe a few feet at a time then you might consider anchoring on a mixture of chain and rope and investing in an anchor bag. This is a heavily made sack with strong handles and large enough to take both the anchor rode and the anchor. When recovering the anchor the rode heaps up in the sack, the anchor goes on top and the whole lot is picked up, taken back to the cockpit and stowed in a locker.

6 Evolutions – Sail Handling

Even in tolerably calm weather the deck of a yacht is an unstable working platform. Taking the way off and turning into the wind to hoist or reef sails can make it very insecure indeed. Heaving-to may be a better option. For your own safety you must always wear a safety harness and be clipped in to a lifeline. Clipping and unclipping to safety lines as you move around the deck can be frustrating. The temptation to speed the action up by not clipping in must be resisted. Falling overboard would really ruin your day. Personal safety and efficiency in sail handling lies in reducing the need to work on deck to a minimum and devising ways of handling sails from the cockpit.

In-boom reefing.

Sail handling determines the minimum number in the crew. Examine your present system and techniques you use and ask how many people are normally needed to safely

- Hoist sails?
- Reef sails?
- Lower, recover and stow sails including a spinnaker if it is carried?

By ignoring risk, taking your time and making a greater than average effort it is possible for one person to handle most sails, but the keyword is 'normally'. If your honest answer exceeds the number of people onboard then you must:

- Abandon plans to sail solo or short-handed, which is unlikely.
- Accept the risks and extra effort of working on deck. This is a reasonable decision. Everyone has a different level of acceptable risk. What scares me witless barely flusters most others. Until about

thirty years ago sail handling had barely changed since the 1920s. Solo sailors managed and although their accounts are full of struggles with reluctant sails they do not include tales of them falling overboard. This is also the cheapest solution.

- Carry fewer sails which will reduce the number of sail changes and therefore the risk and effort. This is a good answer particularly if only one or two sails are giving handling problems. If the spinnaker is the trouble then don't carry one. A spinnaker is a useful but not essential sail. You can always use a boomed-out headsail or a cruising chute as an alternative. This is another cheap solution.
- Modify your sail-handling system. This is not the cheapest answer but it is the most probable solution for most people.
- Go the whole hog and modify your boat's rig which will be time consuming and very expensive.

HEADSAILS

Roller-reefing headsail systems have been around for many years, are well proven, reliable and pretty well universal on cruising boats of all sizes. There is no need to raise and lower headsails and all reefing is done from the cockpit. With little effort it is possible to fit roller reefing to staysails, even boomed-out staysails.

MAIN AND MIZZEN SAILS

For mainsails and mizzen sails slab reefing with lazy jacks works well. It needs no special equipment, and can be rigged out of spare line and blocks, although some commercial versions have their unique selling points. Modern systems use full-length battens and Battcars, which claim to allow the sail to be reefed on any point of sail. One drawback to slab reefing is that compared to a roller-reefing system you have limited choice on how much sail to have up. Three reef points are better than two. The third reef is very deep and after

that there is no need, or desire, to have any sail up.

Slab reefing is quick, simple and reliable. The procedure is:
● slacken halyard;
● partly lower sail;
● haul down the sail and secure tack and clew;
● tighten halyard;
● get back on course;
● tidy up reef points when boat is sailing and more stable. Some proprietary slab-reefing systems make this unnecessary.

Except on the smallest of yachts slab reefing the mainsail is likely to involve some work on deck and it may be that this is a case where it makes nonsense to bring the halyard back to the cockpit. Alternatively it may spark interest in systems that allow mainsail reefing from the cockpit.

Reefing the mainsail by rolling it round the boom was once popular. Reefing was usually

done by going to the mast, inserting a small handle into a worm gear at the gooseneck and cranking forever with one hand while lowering the mainsail with the other. It was necessary to keep some tension on the halyard or creases appeared and ruined the set of the sail. At least one manufacturer (Proctor) developed a system where the reefing handle was on the front of the mast. This gave a 1:1 turn ratio, which was much faster, but you felt very exposed standing with one hand on the reefing handle and the other on the halyard. The main problems with rolling the sail round the boom are:

● battens do not like being rolled up and either have to be coaxed round the boom or removed;
● making a neat roll takes two people, one to lower the sail and one to turn the reefing handle as the sail comes down;
● as more and more sail rolls away the aft end of the boom tends to drop and spoil the set of the sail. This is cured by inserting a

sail bag at the end of the boom as you roll away the sail, and is another example of needing two people;
- there are problems fitting a kicking strap;
- being difficult to hold, especially with cold hands or when wearing gloves, the reefing handle tends to fall overboard. The oceans are littered with them and their loss means problems the next time you reef.

Many years ago I sailed with a gunter rig and the main was reefed by a line which ran along the coachroof and then up to a spindle on the gooseneck. You pulled on this line as you lowered the main and the sail rolled away round the boom. No reefing handle was necessary and I worked from the safety of the cockpit. It still had the problem of the boom dropping as you rolled away sail but in this case could be cured by topping up the gaff. Updated, the same principle is behind today's in-boom reefing systems where the sail disappears onto a roller inside the boom. I do not know if they have solved the problem of the boom dropping. Installing one of these systems involves modifying the gooseneck and replacing the boom. Some also require the adaption of the roach of the mainsail.

In-mast reefing systems apply the principle of headsail roller-reefing systems to mainsails and it can be an add-on or purpose built in the mast. The early versions were little more than a headsail roller-reefing system set up immediately aft of the mast after modifying the gooseneck. Later models attached themselves to the mast, giving it an unusually wide appearance but concealed the foil and rolled up sail. In the latest models the sail disappears inside the mast and gives little hint of its existence. To roll away vertically the mainsail cannot have traditional battens and although the cut of roach allows for this the set of the mainsail and windward performance suffers. Some sails now come with a vertical full-length batten system which is claimed to overcome this disadvantage.

Of all the decisions you make about sail handling, your choice of mainsail systems will be the hardest and is likely to be the most expensive. Each system has its supporters who will hear no criticism of their preference. Those in favour of slab reefing will highlight its simplicity and long-proven track record. In-boom and in-mast supporters will point to the ease with which they handle their sails. Critics will ask, 'What to they do when a sail jams?' Those in favour of in-boom systems hasten to reply they can always lower their mainsail unlike those with in-mast systems. In fact they all work and all have driven yachts many thousands of miles in all kinds of conditions and your choice will, as always, be driven by personal preference and pocket.

You may wish to shorten the mizzen boom to allow a wind vane to be fitted. This means shortening the foot of the sail.

DOWNWIND SAILS

Once when the wind went decently abaft the beam and fell away to a zephyr, the only option, if you wished to continue moving under sail, was to fly a spinnaker. Now the choice includes cruising chutes and gennakers but the solo sailor must use them with care, and for the single-hander hoisting the spinnaker is time consuming.

First, the carefully prepared spinnaker in its bag is brought onto the foredeck and tied down. Next, the sheets and guys are led forward from the cockpit, outside of everything, and attached to the pulpit ready to be clipped onto the pole. Before that can happen you must rig the uphaul and downhaul for the pole and lead their lines back to the cockpit. Next you attach the spinnaker pole to the mast. The bigger the boat, the longer and heavier the spinnaker pole, and fixing one end to the mast is a macho challenge. It can help to attach the uphaul and adjust that to take the weight of the pole. Once the pole is attached to the mast the downhaul and guys can be clipped onto the pole and the sheets to the tack and clew of the spinnaker. Finally the halyard, carefully checked to make sure it is not wrapped round the forestay, is clipped to the head of the sail.

You are now ready to hoist. Ideally you should do this from the cockpit where once the sail is up you have instant control of the sheets and guys. Unfortunately when you wish to drop the sail you need to be on the foredeck to grab it as it comes down, otherwise the spinaker falls into the water and you sail over it. O Joy. On the other hand any delay in controlling the sail once it is hoisted could see it wrapped round the forestay. O Joy of Joys. You pay your money and make your choice.

If you have a snuffer this favours bringing the halyard back to the cockpit. If you do not have a snuffer, think about raising the sail in stops. The easiest way to stop a spinnaker is to cut the bottom off a plastic bucket and slip lots of elastic bands over the bucket. Make sure the sail is not twisted and starting with the head feed the sail through the bucket, slipping an elastic band on the sail every few inches. This turns the sail into a long sausage, which allows you hoist it at the mast and then return to the cockpit where you haul the boom aft and sheet in. This breaks the elastic bands and the sail pops open. Raising the sail in stops still means you must be on the foredeck to lower and recover the sail.

If you wish to gybe a spinnaker then, unless the pole is small enough to be handed round the forestay and the weather kind, you must lower the sail and repeat the entire operation.

The urge to fly a spinnaker comes when the wind is light. Once the sail is up and you swoop along, it is very easy to overlook that the wind has picked up until after a particularly exciting surf you notice a tendency to broach. Too late, you realise that you have a tiger by the tail. It is now time to drop the spinnaker before the boat is completely overpowered. Fully crewed yachts can make a spectacular hash of dropping a spinnaker and you have to do it alone, without a helmsman to keep the boat steady and fully aware that autohelms and windvanes are least efficient on a run.

If you have held on too long then the first task is to slow the boat in an attempt to create a stable working platform. Dropping the mainsail may help and this is where a good mainsail-handling system earns its keep. If you wish to keep the mainsail up to shield the spinnaker then rig a foreguy to the boom before you begin or you may have an uncontrolled gybe when you are working on the foredeck. The next operation is to drop the spinnaker. All you can do is to let the pole go forward so that it lies against the forestay with the sail blowing out ahead. As you go to the mast the boat is slowing down. Loosen the halyard step onto the foredeck and with the halyard clutched in one hand and grab the foot of the sail with the other. Then lower away on the halyard and haul the sail on to the foredeck any way you can. Be prepared for the boat to rock and roll, but with almost all the way off the boat the chances of over running the sail should you drop it in the water are much reduced. Wear gloves for this operation for if the halyard runs away you can suffer a nasty rope burn. At such times investing in a snuffer is an attractive option.

Once the spinnaker is down and secured, put the boat on a steady course and begin tidying away the pole, halyard, uphaul, downhaul, sheets and guys. Then have a cup of tea.

For peace of mind always bring a spinnaker down far, far earlier than you think necessary and certainly long before you would if you had a crew. Once you begin surfing it is too late. Jumping around a rolling foredeck with a halyard in one hand the sail in the other is very dangerous and however inconvenient it may be you must wear a safety harness and be clipped in.

I have heard accounts of solo sailors flying a spinnaker day and night and surviving on brief cap naps. Having once flown a spinnaker for three days I now lack the nerve. I have been taken to task for saying that for the solo sailor a spinnaker is not a cruising sail except in the gentlest of breezes but I shall say it again: it ain't.

Cruising chutes and gennakers significantly improve downwind performance in light airs and have the great advantages that they can be set without a pole and are relatively easy to raise, lower and recover. However, like a spinnaker it is better to recover them early rather than late.

A boomed-out headsail is the poor man's spinnaker. For most cruisers in all but the lightest of winds they are nearly as efficient but far less bother and far safer. The pole should be fitted with an uphaul and downhaul so that it can be controlled. There is also the added advantage than when you boom out a roller-reefing headsail, as the wind speed increases sail area can be reduced by reefing the sail in the normal manner. If necessary, in strong winds the headsail can be rolled away entirely before taking down the pole which by then should be lying quietly close to the forestay. Booming out twin headsails is the traditional ocean crossing rig but it requires a second headsail with its own pole. As this rig needs no mainsail it is possible to use the main boom as a second spinnaker pole. Rig a foreguy to the end of the boom. Next rig a sheet through the end of the boom for your second jib. A snatch block on a shackle beside the mainsheet works well. Hoist the second jib and use the foreguy to pull the boom as near to abeam as it will go. Make the foreguy fast. Sheet in the mainsheet to hold the boom steady and trim the sail.

Some fit a second forestay to carry their second jib but almost any old jib can be set flying on the spinnaker halyard and tacked down to the stemhead fitting. It only needs one sheet and this can be led to the spare track and car of the jib or further aft if you wish. The roller furling headsail is rolled down so that it is the same size as the second jib and the sails are balanced. This rig is stable and easily handled, and works best between a broad reach and a dead run. It also performs over a wide range of wind speeds. As the wind increases it can be converted to a single, boomed-out headsail by rolling away the roller furling jib which is

Working on Mast.

Working on Mast.

a 50% reef. When you roll away the last of the sail let the pole go forward and leave it up. When the wind drops you can return to twin headsails simply by unrolling some sail. All this is done from the cockpit with no more effort than normally reefing a roller headsail.

The effort comes in setting the rig up. This, and taking it down again, takes time and makes it best suited to longer passages. Crossing from the Cape Verde Island to Barbados I carried this rig for twenty days in the north-east Trades and in a Hurley 20 with an 18-foot waterline averaged fractionally under 100 miles a day. Sail handling barely rose above stepping into the cockpit after breakfast and asking myself if I wanted one jib or two. My best day's run was 115 miles noon to noon and for the last few hours as I surfed from one wave to the next I was convinced something would break, but determined to see how well I could do, I hung on to the stroke of noon. Then I rolled the headsail away. The next day, on one loose luffed, boomed-out headsail I made 112 miles!

TACKING

In open water it is possible to tack by setting the new course on the windvane or autohelm. Most autohelms have a tack function, which automatically selects the course. Both windvanes and autohelms are limited in the amount of helm they apply and they will bring the bows round in a gentle, stately arc. This is a far cry from putting the helm hard over and spinning round in a boat length, so plenty of searoom is required. Before starting, check that the headsail sheets are clear and ready to run. Let the main look after itself if it is close hauled otherwise sheet in the main so as to reduce strain on the gooseneck when it comes over. Set the new course on the windvane or autohelm and cast off the lee jib sheet as the bows come through the wind. Haul in as much jib sheet as you can while the sheet is slack and then put it on the winch. Self-tailing winches are helpful but not essential. When the jib is trimmed and set, trim the mainsail.

Climbing the mast.

If there is not enough searoom to tack on the windvane then you must take the helm and put it hard a-lee. Casting off the lee jib sheet as the bows come through the wind is a simple matter; the fun begins hauling the jib sheet in. There is usually a brief instant while the bows are swinging where you can let go of the tiller and use both hands. Afterwards, hold onto the tiller any which way while grinding the sheet in.

GYBING

When you gybe, the first action is to haul the mainsheet in and bring the boom onto the centreline. When this is done then you can wear ship and as the wind goes across the

stern let go and haul the jib sheets. As the boat steadies on its new course then you can check out the mainsheet and set the main.

CLIMBING THE MAST

Climbing the mast at sea should be avoided if at all possible. Except in a flat calm the mast will be swaying to and fro and the higher you go the greater the motion. Lose contact with the mast and you swing out into free space. This is momentarily exhilarating and then you swing back bouncing off first the shrouds and then the mast. There is a good chance of being injured. Keeping the boat moving provides a steadier platform but you must consider the effect your weight

will have on the angle of heel. This varies with height above deck and from boat to boat but it is possible that a gust of wind will lay the boat flat with you tied to the top of the mast.

Although it is often done with two people (one going up and the other working the winch) to be really safe going up the mast is a four-man task:

- One person goes up the mast. He should think about how he is going to keep contact with the mast, particularly when working with both hands. The equipment and tools he takes up with him should include the means of carrying it safely and keeping it attached to him.
- One works the winch that pulls him up.
- One tails the winch.
- One controls the safety line, fed round a second winch and ready to instantly check it in the event of a fall.

Traditionally single-handers used a purchase and bosun's chair to hoist themselves up the mast. Now the choice of mast climbing systems includes:

- Folding ladders which can be hauled up on a spare halyard, which just needs one person working the safety line.
- Steps riveted to the mast which again just needs one person working the safety line.

Bachmann knot

The Bachmann knot is the granddaddy of all slip and grip knots and is superb when used as a safety line when jumaring or being hauled up the mast but as an alternative to jumars it is slow and very fiddly. The Bachmann knot was shown to me by Joe Brown many years ago and is far better but don't use it as a safety line.

First, clip a loop of line into a snap link and pass it through halyard.

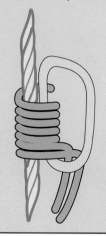

Second, pass the loop at least three times round the halyard AND the snap link. Bring it out through the snap link as shown. The snap link makes a good handle to push or pull up and down the halyard.

- Various gadgets that allow you to climb a halyard by yourself.
- Jumars, sometimes called Cloggers, are gadgets that will slide up a rope but not down. For many years rock climbers used jumars and a sit harness to climb steep, overhanging cliffs. With one jumar clipped to a sit harness and the other to a foot loop you can 'walk' up the mast. This is a well-proven system and since a climbing harness is meant to hold a falling climber there is the reassurance that you can't fall out however much you swing around. Also, since rock climbing demands agility, a climbing harness gives complete freedom of movement, something a bosun's chair, wooden or canvas, cannot offer.

In an emergency it is a simple matter to rig a sit harness out of a loop of rope and to improvise jumars by using a prusik knot or one of its variations. These work, but not as well as the proper kit. If you plan an extended short-handed cruise investing in the correct gear would be wise.

Climbing the mast using jumars and a sit harness is a slow business. You need:

- Jumars
- Sit harness
- One foot loop
- One short safety loop
- Tool bag which always contains a couple of thin loops about three feet long.

Select one halyard for the jumars and another for the safety line. The jumars go one above the other on the halyard. The top jumar clips into your sit harness and the lower jumar carries the foot loop. Push the top jumar as high as it will go. Sit down. Pull the lower jumar to join it. Using the foot loop stand up and simultaneously push the top jumar up the rope. Sit down. Bring the lower jumar up and repeat the cycle until you are as high as you wish to go. Descending, reverse the procedure.

The safety line, clipped to the sit harness, is tied onto a separate halyard by a prusik knot. As you go up the mast it slides up its

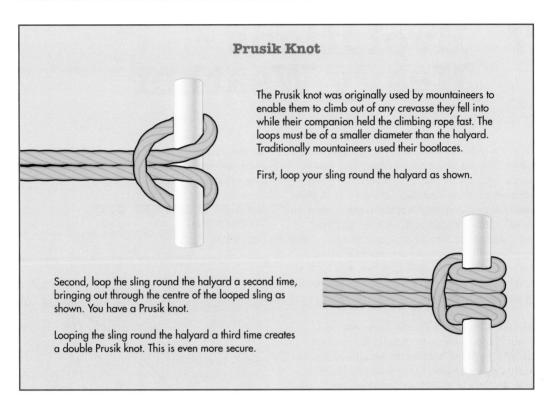

Prusik Knot

The Prusik knot was originally used by mountaineers to enable them to climb out of any crevasse they fell into while their companion held the climbing rope fast. The loops must be of a smaller diameter than the halyard. Traditionally mountaineers used their bootlaces.

First, loop your sling round the halyard as shown.

Second, loop the sling round the halyard a second time, bringing out through the centre of the looped sling as shown. You have a Prusik knot.

Looping the sling round the halyard a third time creates a double Prusik knot. This is even more secure.

halyard. Should your jumar halyard fail then you will fall the length of the safety loop. The prusik knot then tightens and you stop. Once you have recovered your breath, you can, either attach the jumars (if they are within reach) to a new halyard, or fashion a pair of emergency jumars by using the loops carried in the tool bag to tie prusik knots on another halyard and then climb down the mast. It will be slow but far better than hanging around, suspended from a halyard. The short safety loop has the secondary task of holding you into the mast when you are working with both hands.

This sounds far more complicated than it is and a couple of rehearsals in harbour will sort out the kinks. This system is slower than being winched up the mast but has the advantage that you

● can stop, sit down and rest at any time
● are attached to two halyards by independent systems.
● are pushing yourself up by your legs and not hauling yourself up by your arms.

Regardless of which one-man mast-climbing system you choose it is far, far better not to have to climb the mast at all. You can reduce the chance of having to go up the mast at sea by fitting the following spares:

● halyards with at least one on the front of the mast and another aft of the mast. The topping lift can be pressed into use as a halyard. Do not count it as one of your spares.
● navigation lights in a position where they can be reached from the deck. These may be small, battery-operated lights which clip onto shrouds, or if you have a radar scanner or wind generator on a pole why not hard wire a spare tri-colour light on top of the pole?
● aerials in a position where they can be reached from the deck. This is more difficult. A goalpost on the stern is ideal for carrying all sorts of odds and ends. Lacking that, an emergency VHF can, if its cable is long enough, be hoisted on a signal halyard. Its range will be decreased but it will work.

7 Evolutions – Heavy Weather

Heavy weather is hard on the single-handed sailor. You are never certain how long a gale will last. It may be hours or days. Even pacing yourself from the start there comes a time when rest is scarce and fatigue is a serious danger. Initially strong winds and big seas may be exhilarating but fatigue, motion and noise erode morale until all you want is a moment's peace and quiet to pull yourself together, and for that brief pleasure you will gladly accept the devil's invitation to supper.

Bad weather rarely arrives unannounced. Even without access to regular forecasts the behaviour of the barometer and the sky gives a reliable indication of the weather to come, and the time to start your preparations to meet bad weather is when you see the first signs of its approach. Should the bad weather not materialise then your preparations count as useful practice.

In heavy weather every task, however simple, becomes more difficult and time consuming. There is an understandable reluctance to work on a cold wet deck, no desire to linger in a wind-strewn cockpit. The temptation of repeatedly delaying tasks for just a minute is the primrose path to problems that must be ignored and never taken. On fully crewed yachts the workload, effort and misery is shared. On a short-handed or single-handed boat they grind you down and can overwhelm the crew. So, prepare early when the weather is relatively calm and working is easy.

When your preparations are complete, then rest. A real danger is that having done all that can be done your worries and concerns drive you to look for something else to do. You waste energy on unnecessary work. As a general rule ships handle heavy weather better than their crews. Their motion can be alarming, the seas terrifying, and the wind sound like a demented

dervish on speed but well prepared ships will come through with only minimal assistance from their crew.

HEAVY WEATHER OFF SOUNDINGS
Heaving-to

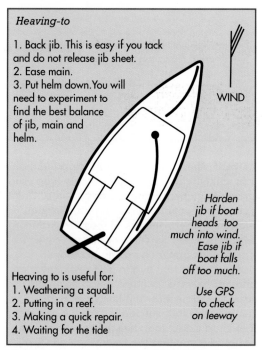

Heaving-to

1. Back jib. This is easy if you tack and do not release jib sheet.
2. Ease main.
3. Put helm down. You will need to experiment to find the best balance of jib, main and helm.

WIND

Harden jib if boat heads too much into wind. Ease jib if boat falls off too much.

Use GPS to check on leeway

Heaving to is useful for:
1. Weathering a squall.
2. Putting in a reef.
3. Making a quick repair.
4. Waiting for the tide

If you are far off soundings with unlimited searoom then you can try heaving-to. Traditionally yachts heaved-to by sheeting in the main and backing the jib. With helm tied down they then would forereach, head more or less to wind and seas, making some leeway but not going anywhere in particular. The right balance of jib and main is important and this varies with wind strength. Too much sail and the immediate result is a frightening angle of heel. Use the absolute minimum amount of sail from the outset. Some yachts will heave-to under jib alone; others may need a scrap of main.

HEAVY WEATHER CHECKLIST

SERIAL	ACTION
1	Bring your navigation up to date.
2	Decide on your heavy weather strategy eg divert to a harbour of refuge, or if that is not possible when to start by heaving-to, going to cork mode, or if these actions are not an option then deciding when to run before the weather, or lie to sea anchor.
3	Calculate the wind strengths and sea states when you will move one element of your planned heavy weather strategy to the next and note this down in the log.
4	If you intend to stream warps then make sure they and all their anti-chafe materials are to hand in a convenient locker. The same applies to sea anchors and drogues if you plan to use them.
5	Check stowage arrangements. Stowage that is fine in normal weather can have the cabin full of flying objects that could hurt you.
6	Dig out your warm clothing, oilskins, seaboots, harness and lifejacket and put them on.
7	Check the crash bag is to hand and fully packed with all you need.
8	Check the liferaft is secure.
9	Check all halyards and lines are secure and not going to either untie themselves or let their tails blow out in the wind.
10	Check every item of equipment on deck is secure. This includes dinghies, lifebuoys, danbuoys and their lights.
11	If you drop the mainsail and tie it to the boom then plan to do this before working on deck becomes a desperate business. Makes sure the sail is secure. Use additional sail ties to make sure the sail cannot blow free.
12	If you plan to use either a trysail and/or storm jib then these must be rigged early rather than late.
13	If you have hanks on headsails then do not tie unwanted headsails to the guardrail. Bring them below or stow them in a cockpit locker.
14	Pump the bilges.
15	Top up fuel tanks, you might wish to run the engine and filling tanks in heavy weather is a nightmare.
16	Turn off all seacocks that are not immediately required.
17	Top up your ready-to-use food supplies.
18	Feed the crew before the bad weather arrives.
19	Prepare food and drink for during the heavy weather. If you like having hot drinks and soups in flasks then prepare them when the weather is calm. A hot meal such as an all-in stew, prepared in a pressure cooker which is allowed to cool without taking the pressure off is effectively canned and will keep for several days. In prolonged heavy weather this ready cooked all-in stew can be brought out and heated up with the minimum of effort to provide a good, nourishing meal. In extremis it can be eaten cold. I like have lots of nibbles and easy to prepare hot drinks. For me variety is important. Sometimes soup is the drink of choice, at others, hot chocolate, coffee or tea. There are times when I want savoury nibbles, at others only sweets. Unless you absolutely sure of how your taste buds perform, carry a wide selection.
20	Monitor weather forecasts and the barometer.
21	Make a final check that all above and below decks is in order.

Heaving-to is fine until the wind increases to a level where it is beginning to overpower your boat and laying it over almost onto its beam ends. At this point, when working on deck is extremely hazardous, it will be necessary to take down the sails and consider some other option or run for your life. If the forecast winds are expected to reach a level where your boat will be overpowered when hove-to, then either take all sail down earlier than you would otherwise or adopt some other option from the start.

Heaving-to works best for long-keeled yachts. Fin and skeg boats or those with spade rudders and deep narrow keels may heave-to almost broadside to the seas or not heave-to at all. Experiment with different sail plans and rudder settings to find out if your boat heaves-to, preferably beginning in gentle winds and easy seas.

Keep track of your drift when hove-to by setting the anchor alarm on the GPS to a range that keeps you well clear of any dangers, by at least two or three miles. If you doze then the alarm will ring long before you are in trouble. The GPS will also display your course and speed made good and this can be run forward to check that you stay well clear of any hazards.

THE CORK MODE

The cork mode is a good option provided there is plenty of searoom. The bows are pointed about 60^0 off the wind and the wind vane set to hold that course. With a tiny scrap of jib sheeted in hard, or even no jib at all, you plod slowly upwind with bare steerage way. Like heaving-to, the wind and seas are taken just aft of the bow, but compared to the speed of the advancing waves your boat is relatively motionless and like a cork rises up the front of the wave and slides slowly down it back. Even in breaking seas this is surprisingly comfortable. The problem comes from rogue waves travelling against the dominant wave front. If they hit, then your boat is likely to be shoved sideways before picking herself up and resuming her cork mode.

The cork mode works because off soundings the waves are enormously long. There are six

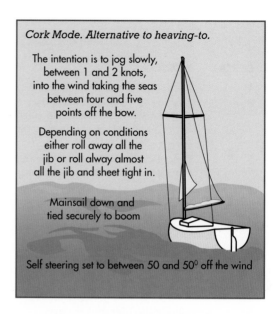

Cork Mode. Alternative to heaving-to.

The intention is to jog slowly, between 1 and 2 knots, into the wind taking the seas between four and five points off the bow.

Depending on conditions either roll away all the jib or roll alway almost all the jib and sheet tight in.

Mainsail down and tied securely to boom

Self steering set to between 50 and 50^0 off the wind

to eight seconds crest to crest, and although they are many feet high their gradient is gentle so that your boat always has way on and sails up and down the waves. This holds her position relative to winds and seas and provides a fairly steady platform. In this mode it is possible to make anything between thirty to fifty miles up wind in a day and this should be factored into your decision to adopt the cork mode.

LYING A-HULL

Lying a-hull, sometimes called lying a-try, is nothing more than taking all sails down, tying the helm down and leaving the boat to look after itself. I have only tried this once or twice and do not like it. The boat tends to lie across the waves. The motion was horrendous and on the two or three occasions I have tried lying a-hull I could not rid myself of the worry that lying broadside to a breaking wave carried the promise of an a knockdown or a total inversion.

RUNNING

Running away from bad weather is probably the most comfortable option but only if there is sufficient searoom, and preferably if you are travelling in the right direction. It is best to run away slowly as sailing too fast carries the danger of surfing and broaching. In heavy weather this must be avoided. In strong winds

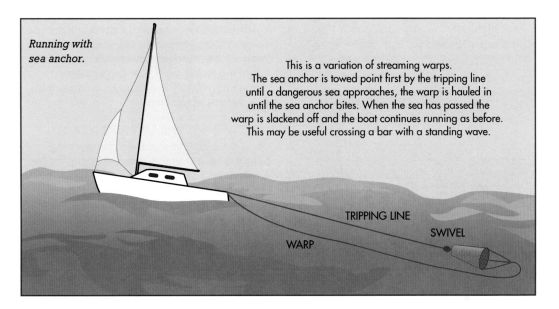

Running with sea anchor.

This is a variation of streaming warps. The sea anchor is towed point first by the tripping line until a dangerous sea approaches, the warp is hauled in until the sea anchor bites. When the sea has passed the warp is slackend off and the boat continues running as before. This may be useful crossing a bar with a standing wave.

TRIPPING LINE

SWIVEL

WARP

it is possible to travel too fast even under bare poles. If so, consider streaming warps. Their drag will not only slow the boat but will steady it on its course and even help create a slick of calmer water astern.

STORM SAILS

Storm sails are a traditional response to heavy weather when the usual rig is storm jib and trysail. A storm jib is made of very heavy material with reinforcements at the head, clew and tack to withstand the inevitable misuse. Nowadays they are often of orange coloured material to improve visibility. The biggest problem in setting a storm jib is that most yachts have rolling-reefing headsails and there is no stay onto which the storm jib can be hanked. You can remove the roller-reefing headsail and hoist the storm jib in the track instead. If this is to be done then do it before conditions make working on deck hazardous and with modern sailmaking materials the end result is probably no better than rolling away most of the headsail. Alternatively you can set the storm jib flying, which means finding some strong point for the tack and a spare halyard to hoist it. Set flying you abandon all hope that you may have had of any upwind progress and if later it is necessary to lie a-hull or run under bare poles then you must go on to the foredeck in truly horrible conditions and take it down.

To rig a trysail the main is dropped and either secured to the boom or taken off entirely. Then the boom is lowered on its topping lift and made fast and the mainsheet removed. In the days when every boom came with its own gallows this was a simple operation. Now booms lie across the coachroof and cockpit, lashed to the guardrail and blocking access to the sidedecks. It is very unsatisfactory.

The mainsheet is attached to the trysail and then this is hoisted either using the same track as the mainsail or in its own track. Normally the mainsail halyard is used. It is boomless with the intention of taking the strain off the gooseneck and removing the risk of anyone being hit by a flailing boom but, like a storm jib, it removes any possibility of upwind progress. Again, the effort involved in hoisting a trysail means that the work must carried out early before the weather makes working on deck dangerous.

DROGUES AND SEA ANCHORS

A drogue is towed astern when running to slow the yacht down and reduces the risk of pitch poling, surfing or broaching. A sea anchor is also used to bring the bows into the seas and reduce drift when lying a-hull. It should be at least one wave length out from the bows and given the long wavelengths off soundings this requires lots and lots of warp.

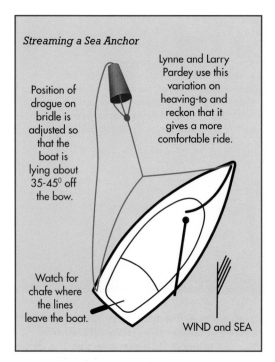

Streaming a Sea Anchor

Position of drogue on bridle is adjusted so that the boat is lying about 35-45° off the bow.

Lynne and Larry Pardey use this variation on heaving-to and reckon that it gives a more comfortable ride.

Watch for chafe where the lines leave the boat.

WIND and SEA

I have carried a traditional canvas sea anchor and a modern parachute sea anchor for many thousands of miles and never used either. There are many good reports of boats successfully riding out extreme weather using a parachute sea anchor.

CREW AND HEAVY WEATHER

Once the boat has steadied down and is happy then it is time to take shelter. The best place is your bunk. This is when decent lee cloths allow you to curl up without any fear of falling out of bed. Val Howells, who took part in the first two or three single-handed trans-Atlantic races in a Folkboat, carried flagons of his grandmother's home-made knockout brew. In bad weather he would drink till he fell asleep. When he woke he would look out; if it was still blowing he drank some more.

It is as good an answer as any. Off soundings and out of shipping lanes the chances of meeting another vessel are very low. Sitting in the cockpit for hours on end in bad weather reduces you to a zombie. Mentally your thought processes would be too sluggish to make a sensible appreciation of the situation. If there is an emergency you are unlikely to make a prompt, intelligent response. Physical movement would be difficult and your numbed fingers would be unable to tie, or untie knots. You are much more likely to handle problems coming out of a warm and comfortable bunk.

It also needs very strong cleats to carry the very high loads. If in doubt bring the line to the mast. Chafe is a huge problem with both drogues and sea anchors.

It is possible that with a sea anchor out your boat will lie, not bows to the sea as expected, but take the seas somewhere between the bows and amidships. It is also possible for sternway to develop and this will impose heavy loads on the rudder which could damage it.

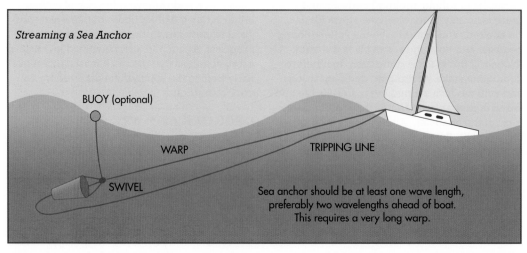

Streaming a Sea Anchor

BUOY (optional)

WARP

TRIPPING LINE

SWIVEL

Sea anchor should be at least one wave length, preferably two wavelengths ahead of boat. This requires a very long warp.

HEAVY WEATHER IN COASTAL WATERS

If there is sufficient warning of bad weather then there is no doubt that the best place to sit out a gale is the nearest yacht club bar. If you are in port then stay there even if the delay inconveniences yourself or others. If you are on passage and cannot reach your destination in time, then divert early for a harbour of refuge so as to arrive before the weather turns. If the bad weather does not materialise then you have simply added another port to your itinerary. Avoiding bad weather is sensible and prudent.

A suitable harbour of refuge may be some distance off and take many hours sailing in worsening weather to reach. With the washboards in and hatches closed, leaving the cockpit is a rare event. It helps to have stocks of nibbles and flasks in the cockpit along with charts, GPS, torches and a couple of white flares. If you cannot reach your destination or a harbour of refuge then you must stay out at sea. This is easier to advise than achieve. It will almost certainly demand prolonged and continuous effort. Finding sufficient searoom to sit out a gale in coastal waters is difficult unless the strong winds are of very short duration.

A course must be laid to keep you clear of dangers. These include not just the obvious hazards but also shoals and shallows that can become ship-killing overfalls in heavy weather. In shipping lanes small boats will be invisible to both the eye and to radar, and your ability to avoid other traffic is severely limited.

Despite barside claims of superb windward performance in full gales and skippers standing at the helm effortlessly shedding water from their stiff upper lip for hours on end, you must face facts and take into account that in heavy weather your vessel's upwind performance, like yours, will be severely degraded. You may have to consider motor-sailing to make any forward movement. Even then progress is likely to be painfully slow and extremely uncomfortable. In coastal waters the seas have short wavelengths and boats fall off one wave and into the next. This takes way off and knocks the boat sideways. Leeway is so horrendous that the course made good is almost at right angles to the course steered. Genuine windward progress becomes an illusion.

If you must sail off a lee shore then, regardless of where your destination lies, choose the tack that points furthest offshore. Take great care when you tack not to miss stays and lose all the ground won on that tack, and above all, keep the boat moving as fast as possible. If necessary, sail a little free rather than close hauled and pinching in an effort to claim every possible windward yard. Leeway will be prodigious and some luck will be needed to win this challenge.

Luck is useful but it is unreliable and for this reason, unless it is necessary to fight your way off a lee shore or escape some other danger, it is best not to include going to windward in your coastal waters heavy-weather strategy. Most boats sink when they hit something and they most commonly collide with land. Staying far out at sea and waiting for better weather appears perverse but it does lessen the chance of a confrontation with mother earth.

Spending most of your time in the cockpit it, is important to be well wrapped up. You must stay warm and dry. Have a stock of dry towels and scarves to slow down water seeping in around your neck and gradually soaking you. It is inevitable that you will become wet but try to delay it as long as possible. Warm wet is an illusion. You are losing body heat warming cold water.

You may yearn to be in harbour but approaching the shore can be extremely hazardous. The objective dangers increase in both in number and proximity. Closing the coast can be very committing and returning offshore difficult or impossible. The nearer the shore the fewer the options open to you. You will be tired and your judgement coloured by the nearness of the harbour's promised peace and quiet. It is essential to confirm your position before committing yourself to leaving the safety of the open sea and heading for the harbour. If possible, call the harbourmaster on the VHF and check if it is safe to enter. In a near gale in the Moray Firth we asked Buckie's harbourmaster for his opinion of conditions in the harbour and its approaches, and received the reply that we were welcome to come in but should know that the fishing boats were not going out. We took the hint and ran back to Fraserburgh.

RESTRICTED VISIBILITY

Every yacht, fully, short crewed or single-handed is at danger in restricted visibility. Commercial shipping appears to have abandoned slowing down and making sound signals in fog, relying instead on a radar watch. Yachts give a poor radar return, even with a radar reflector, and are often lost in sea clutter. In short, commercial vessels do not know of your existence and if they run you down they would not feel the bump.

For any pleasure craft in busy waters this is a time of extreme danger. Without radar or the electrical power to run it, your safety depends on other vessels keeping out of your way, not you keeping out of theirs. Announce your presence by transmitting an all-ships security message giving your position, course and speed every fifteen or twenty minutes. This may encourage other vessels to take a closer look at their radar screen. Holding a steady course and speed is important. When you appear on another vessel's radar they will plot your point of closest approach (CAP) which assumes you maintain a steady course and speed. Tacking and weaving around ought not to confuse the machine, for modern radars automatically update the CAP, but it is possible the OOW will miss this information. If necessary think about starting the engine to hold a steady course.

If you have any electronic watch-keeping aids such as radar, radar detector, AIS or radar target enhancers then use them. Regardless of time of day it is usual to switch on your ship's navigation lights in poor visiblity. This is no more than a gesture. A strobe may be visible further but its light can bounce back of the fog and blind you, particularly at night.

It is wise to stay in the cockpit, dress warmly and wear oilskins and a lifejacket. Think carefully before wearing a safety harness and clipping on. Can you be sure of unclipping if

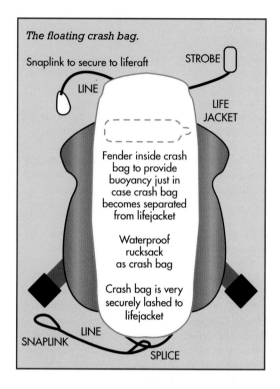

The floating crash bag.

Snaplink to secure to liferaft

STROBE

LINE

LIFE JACKET

Fender inside crash bag to provide buoyancy just in case crash bag becomes separated from lifejacket

Waterproof rucksack as crash bag

Crash bag is very securely lashed to lifejacket

SNAPLINK   LINE

SPLICE

you do collide with another vessel and have to abandon ship? Think even more carefully before going below. You may be certain that you will be able to fight your way out on deck if there is a collision while you are below. The probability is that you will not.

Consider inflating and towing the dinghy. In the event of a collision there may not be time to launch the life raft. The dinghy may represent the last chance saloon for anyone wishing to stay afloat. If you do tow the dinghy make sure you, and everyone else aboard, has a sharp knife in their pocket to cut the line.

ABANDONING SHIP

This is only done when every other option is closed and sinking is both inevitable and imminent. Practise the abandon ship before hand until everyone knows what to do and how to do it without thinking or asking stupid questions. This applies as much to the single-hander as the fully crewed ship. Rehearsing your abandon-ship drill highlights those areas where theory and practice collide. Knowing the order in which tasks are to be carried out is as important as knowing what has to be done.

If you sail with a crew make your mind up who does what and make sure they know their area of responsibility and how it fits into the overall plan. On short-handed craft more work falls on fewer people. For the family cruiser of Mum, Dad and two kids, one parent will be looking after the children while the other sorts out abandoning ship.

Decide who is responsible for:
- Sending out the Mayday message...one person should be working the radio until you leave the ship.
- Checking everyone is wearing extra clothing (including a hat), oilskins, lifejackets, harnesses.
- Having crash bag to hand and that it goes in the liferaft. The crashbag's contents will vary whether inshore (short-term survival) or offshore (long-term survival).

When it comes to leave the boat it is not every man for themselves. The skipper must decide beforehand the order in which the crew leave the ship. It may be necessary for someone who is fit and can be relied upon to behave sensibly to enter the liferaft first and help the others aboard until the skipper joins them. It is a privilege of rank for skippers to leave sinking ships after the crew but before the rats.

THE CRASH BAG

ITEM	QUANTITY	REMARKS
Handheld VHF		Battery fully charged before casting off.
Handheld GPS		Programme the GPS with the way points for that passage and include a list of other useful waypoints.
A small-scale chart		Covering the entire area of proposed passage.
Compass		A small Silva marching type compass is perfectly adequate.
Torch		Must be completely waterproof.
Knife		A multi-tool knife is a good choice.
Flares		These are to supplement those in the liferaft pack and should be a mixture of smoke, handheld red, and red parachute flares.
Strobe lights		Small battery powered strobes are reasonably inexpensive.
Heliograph		
Spare batteries for GPS/torch/strobe		These should be replaced regularly.
Ship's papers		Including details of insurance policy.
Your papers including credit cards/passports		It is a good idea to stow these in a waterproof map case.
Additional food, water and first aid.		
One-time exposure suits		At least one for everyone on board.

For long-term survival you might to consider adding:
- Handheld water maker. A solar still is an alternative. Both are expensive.
- Fishing tackle.
- More water in plastic jerry cans. Every can must be clipped to the raft.
- More food.

The crash bag must float. It may be all that stands between you and staying alive. Give it its own lifejacket and strobe for abandoning ship at night. The crash bag must be attached to the liferaft at all times. This is one of the occasions I would not trust anyone (including me) to tie a secure knot first time. My crash bag has a line with a snaplink on one end that I can clip in one handed if necessary.

8 Evolutions – Berthing

Berthing is a demanding time for the short-handed sailor. At first, a gale may appear more challenging but during heavy weather it is nearly always possible to stop and think before you act. You control the pace at which proceedings happen. In berthing, once an action is begun you must keep up with events. Harbours and marinas are busy, crowded places. Distances are short, often measured in boat lengths. Manoeuvring space is limited and margins of error are small. There is rarely sufficient time to recover from an unexpected miscalculation before colliding with some other boat or the pontoon.

Having a crew, even a crew of one, makes everything much easier. They can fend off other boats, keep a lookout, stand midships and step ashore with the lines as you come alongside, or tend to the bow warp while you look after the stern lines as you enter a box. If you have a crew, then before you begin your berthing manoeuvres always take the time to brief them on what you plan to do and who does what. Before doing anything, hang around, take a good look where you intend to berth, and work out exactly what you are going to do before you start the berthing sequence.

The four golden rules are:
1. Always select the easiest berth to enter even if it is not the most convenient for the yacht club bar.
2. Never refuse assistance from those onshore. If you foresee problems and can manage to look completely incompetent, then driven by self-preservation, crews from your neighbours-to-be will offer to assist. Otherwise do not be slow to ask for help.
3. Always plan your approach beforehand.
4. Do not change your mind at the last minute. Some of my better contretemps have been caused by having a better idea too late. At slow speeds in very confined waters, rapid and dramatic changes in course or speed (or both) are not possible.

When you come alongside it is not a good notion to leap ashore and then begin looking for somewhere to secure your line. Once alongside wind and tide will soon have your boat moving and you will find yourself in a tug of war with several tons of boat. The chances are you will lose. Always identify the mooring points you wish to use before going alongside. The usual choice is from cleats, bollards, rings, and piles and each requires a slightly different way of preparing the lines before you go ashore.

CLEATS
Checking the way on your boat and making fast to an empty cleat is straightforward, and

Busy Cleats

Closed Ring Cleat

Cleats and Springs.   *Cleats on pontoon.*   *Closed Cleat.*

in diagrams they are always shown empty apart from your line. In real life they are often fully occupied by other ropes and once you have checked the way on your boat, throwing on a clove hitch can provide a quick, temporary solution to the problem of how to make fast while you sort out the other lines. Later, when you are tidying up the lines and find that you cannot make your line fast to the cleat without it capsizing, then a bowline hauled tight is probably best.

BOLLARDS
Always have more capacity than cleats. Making fast with a round turn and two half-hitches is better than going ashore with a ready made bowline which may or may not fit, although it is a neater solution when you tidy up the lines.

RINGS
Some rings are attached to eyebolts and lie flat to a wall or the ground. Consequently they must be held in one hand while the other

Bollard.

Bollards in Lock.

Lock Eider.   *Lock Eider Using Ladder.*   *Lock Eider using Ladder and Bollard.*

Pile with Mooring Ring

Piles as Bollards

Piles Eider MBoats

Piles, Lines

feeds the rope through; others stand upright and resemble a closed cleat. In both cases securing to them can involve hauling through several miles of rope. This can be difficult if you are holding a line in each hand and the wind is blowing hard. The easiest solution is to pull through a bight long enough for a couple of half hitches, which will hold the boat while you sort out the other lines.

LADDERS

Ladders are generally found on harbour walls, wooden stagings, and locks and like mooring bollards or rings always out of reach. It is impossible to safely climb a ladder carrying mooring lines. The risk of being hauled off is too great. Try standing midships and make the bow and stern lines fast to an easily reached rung with a round turn and two half hitches. Once that is done you can climb the ladder and take other mooring lines ashore one at a time.

PILES

How you put a line round a pile depends on its height, which can vary with the tide. It is a

simple matter to throw a bight of rope round a low pile but for high piles it may be easier to tie a large bowline in the end of the line and drop it over the pile with the help of a boathook. Passing a line round a pile from the boat needs a very thin pile or you may leave the boat hugging the pile. Some piles have an arrangement so that lines are threaded through a ring which rises and falls with the tide. It is often impossible to make fast to the ring as you enter the box and you must be prepared to throw a line round the pile and sort it out afterwards.

Tide Rip on Pontoons.
Never assume there is no tide in marinas.

Berthing Alongside a Quay

STEP ONE

1. In clear water prepare warps and fenders for berthing.
2. Approach heading into the wind or tide whichever is the stronger.
3. Check out the berth first. Know where you are going to make your shore line fast before going alongside.
4. Always maintain steerageway. Check your progress by making transits out of nearby features on shore. Approaches always seem too slow right up until the last minute when you wonder how on earth you will stop in time.

STEP TWO

1. As you come into the quay put the helm over and give a burst ahead to straighten up.
2. Almost immediately you may need to go astern to take the way off and come to a stop. Remember to pause for an instant in neutral when going from ahead to astern.

STEP THREE

1. Pick up the lines.
2. Go midships.
3. Step ashore.
4. You have a choice, you can use the
(a) bow line as a forespring and drop back a little when bow line is fast make the stern warp fast or
(b) stern line as a backspring and not drop back at all when backspring is fast make the bow warp fast.
5. This secures your boat and you have time to add warps and springs as necessary.

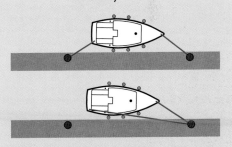

Berthing Alongside Another Boat

STEP ONE

1. Berthing alongside another yacht is very similar to going alongside a quay but remember
(a) their cleats may be already in use or inadequate
(b) they may not have fenders out
(c) getting aboard may not be straightforward
(d) to make sure masts are not 'abeam'.
2. Select a boat about the same size as your boat.
3. Adjust the height of your fenders to suit.
4. If there is anyone aboard ask permission to come alongside. They will probably help by taking your lines.
5. Approach as you would alongside a quay.

STEP TWO

1. Come alongside.
2. Stop your boat.
3. If there is no-one to take your lines, pick them up, go midships and climb aboard. Shrouds make a useful handhold.
4. Use your stern line as a back-spring. If there is nothing else then tie it off to a shroud.
5. Make your bow line fast.
6. Your boat is now secure and you can finish putting on warps, springs and shore lines.

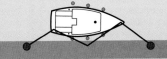

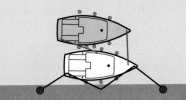

Entering a finger pontoon with cross wind and tide

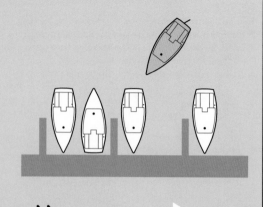

STEP ONE
1. In clear water prepare warps and fenders port and starboard.
2. Approach berth aiming off for the effects of wind and tide.
3. This usually means aiming for the stern of the boat next door.
4. If you need put the helm over and give a burst ahead to increase your rate of turn then do so early rather than late.

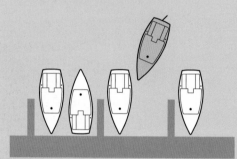

STEP TWO
1. You should be straightening up to enter your berth.
2. If you are approaching too fast put the engine astern to slow down. Make sure the bows continue to swing round.

STEP THREE
1. You are now committed to entering the berth.
2. The engine should be in neutral allowing you to enter under the boat's residual way.
3. The effect of the rudder is less pronounced at slow speeds and attempting to increase the rate of turn by putting the rudder hard over will only slow the boat down.
4. If the boat has stopped swinging the easiest way to straight up is to go forward with the boathook and push off the neighbouring boat.

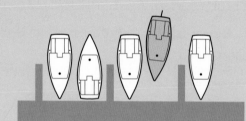

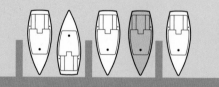

STEP FOUR
1. Let wind and tide carry your boat onto the finger pontoon.
2. Pick up the lines.
3. Step ashore.
4. Make fast lines.

Entering a finger pontoon with wind and tide coming from astern

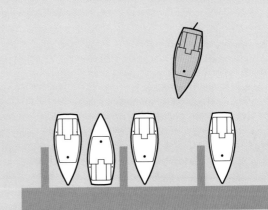

STEP ONE

1. In clear water prepare warps and fenders for berthing.
2. As you approach your berth put the helm over and give short bursts ahead on the engine until you are pointing more or less directly at your berth.

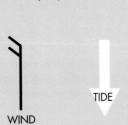

WIND   TIDE

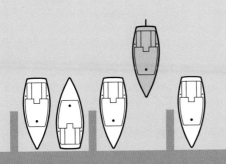

STEP TWO

1. Let the wind and tide carry you into your berth.
2. Watch your speed. The aim is to be going fast enough to keep steerage way and slow enough to stop before hitting the main pontoon.
3. If necessary put the engine astern to slow down.

STEP THREE

1. As you reach the finger pontoon give a final burst astern to bring the boat to a complete stop.
2. Throw the stern warp across the finger pontoon.
3. Go ashore carrying the bow warp and use that as a backspring to hold the bows off the main pontoon.
4. Pick up the stern warp and make it fast to stop the stern swinging out. (You threw it ashore because making one warp fast while holding another is really awkward.)
5. Finish securing warps and springs.

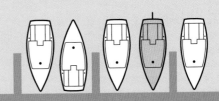

Entering a finger pontoon with cross wind and tide (2)

STEP ONE
1. In clear water prepare warps and fenders for berthing.
2. As you approach your berth put the helm over and give short bursts ahead on the engine until you are pointing more or less directly at your berth.

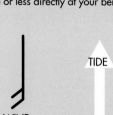

WIND   TIDE

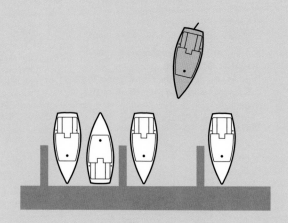

STEP TWO
1. Motor slowly into berth.
2. The wind and tide will slow you down so be sure to maintain steerage way.

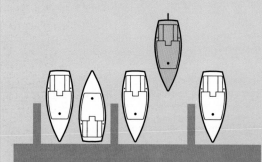

STEP THREE
1. As you reach the finger pontoon give a final burst astern to bring the boat to a complete stop. With luck this will be unnecessary.
2. Throw the bow warp across the finger pontoon.
3. Go ashore carrying the stern warp and use that as a backspring to hold the bows off the main pontoon.
4. Pick up the bow warp and make it fast to stop the bows swinging out. (You threw it ashore because making one warp fast while holding another is really awkward.)
5. Finish securing warps and springs.

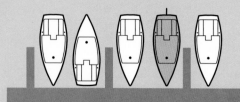

Entering a Pontoon Berth in Cross Wind and Tide

STEP ONE
1. Entering a pontoon berth in cross wind and tide is never straightforward, particularly if turning space is limited.
2. Start your turn early by putting the helm over and giving brief bursts ahead on the engine.
3. If you complete your turn early then let wind and tide carry you sideways.

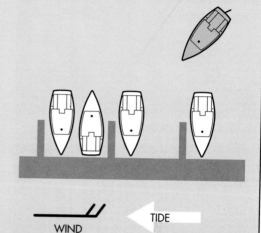

WIND   TIDE

STEP TWO
1. If it looks like you will reach your berth before completing your turn then slow down. If necessary go astern.
2. Once stopped, or almost so, put the helm over and give short bursts ahead on the engine to swing the bows round with minimal forward motion.

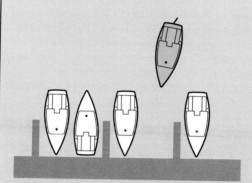

STEP THREE
1. You may find that you are almost crabbing into your berth but putting the helm midships at the right moment should straighten your approach.
2. You must keep steerage way as you enter the pontoon.

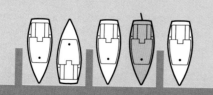

STEP FOUR
1. As you reach the finger pontoon give a burst astern to take the way off and bring boat to a complete stop.
2. Throw the bow warp across the finger pontoon.
3. Step ashore with the stern warp and make that fast to prevent the stern swinging out.
4. Make the bow warp fast.
5. Complete making warps and springs fast.

Oostmahorn Jacht Hafen.

Drying Berths.

Pontoon Berth.

GOING ALONGSIDE

Coming alongside a pontoon or a wall and stopping is not normally a problem. Troubles begin in the interval between coming alongside, stopping and taking the lines ashore. In calm conditions with little or no tide the problems are insignificant. The boat stays where you put it and you can step ashore and make up the lines with all the time in the world. In strong winds and currents the problems are horrendous. There are only seconds to reach the shore and make at least one line fast before the elements take control of your boat but even in the worst conditions there is a brief instant when your boat is lying nicely alongside before the wind and tide take charge.

The key to success is to take advantage of this lull to grab the lines and step ashore. Controlled speed is essential. If you know that you will be making up the bow (or stern) line

first fling the other line ashore so that you have only one line to carry. In most conditions the first line made fast acts as a spring. Tie it off and then deal with the other line you have thrown ashore. A line made fast to a cleat amidships can be used as either a fore or stern spring as the situation demands. If you do rig a midships line then fling the bow and stern warps ashore, and step onto the pontoon holding the midships spring, make it fast and then turn your attention to the bow and stern warps.

Leaping onto a pontoon is normally no problem. Difficulties begin when you lie alongside a wall or staging and must climb a ladder to reach the bollards or cleats or whatever is available to secure your lines. It is not easy climbing a ladder holding lines while the wind and tide have control of your boat which is trying to drag you off. The easy answer is to make temporary lines fast to the ladder before you climb ashore with your lines. Your boat may not lie neatly to the wall but at least it is not attempting to pull you into the sea.

Sometimes it is necessary to lie to a much larger vessel. Fortunately most comercial vessels have a good choice of strong fittings which will happily accept a yacht's lines. Otherwise it is, for example, usually possible to make fast to their stanchions or guardrails, not something you can do to another yacht without causing damage.

I have seen a single-hander stand in the cockpit, drop his midships spring over a cleat and, leaving way on, use it as a spring to hold his boat quietly alongside the pontoon while he sorted out his other lines with all the time in the

Laying to Barge.

world. It was an impressive performance but my efforts to emulate it have proved crowd-pulling, comic failures. Two points to remember if you wish to try this manoeuvre: first there must be a cleat or a bollard to drop the bowline over (rings are no use); second, you must have some means of adjusting the spring from the cockpit so that it is the correct length.

BERTHING BETWEEN BOATS
It is common to berth between two boats lying

Berthed between two boats.

to a hammerhead or long pontoon. How you do so depends largely on the space between the two berthed vessels. If the gap is more than three boats lengths then it is possible to approach at an angle that brings your boat alongside and allows you to step ashore with the lines. Nearly always the first priority is to put a spring on to prevent you blowing down onto one of the other boats. A midships warp makes a good spring, and once that is fast the bow and stern warps will pull your boat nicely alongside. Once secure there is then time to decide if you wish to move your boat closer to one of the other boats.

Less than three boat lengths between the berthed vessels means that the approach angle is so steep that at the last moment you must put the helm hard over and give a burst of power to the engine to swing the stern in. As soon as that happens you must go astern to take the way off before hitting the boat ahead. In the few seconds between coming alongside and gathering sternway it is vital to put a spring ashore to avoid dropping back onto the vessel astern.

BERTHING IN A BOX
A box is a berth where you put stern lines out to piles and lie bows to a pontoon which may, or may not, have short finger pontoons between berths. Sometimes there is a line strung between piles and the pontoon, and this may prevent you blowing down onto another boat. Boxes come in different sizes

Some marinas offer a choice of berthing alongside or going into a box. Where possible choose to go alongside.

Berthing Between Boats

STEP ONE

1. When the gap between berthed boats is over two or three boat lengths come alongside as normal.

2. For smaller gaps:

(a) In clear water prepare warps and fenders for coming alongside.

(b) Take a close look at your berth. Know where you will make your lines fast.

(c) Approach upwind or uptide whichever is the stronger.

(d) Select an aiming point so that your stern will clear the bows of Boat A, miss the stern of Boat B and give you enough room to swing alongside. It may help to fix this point by using onshore features as a transit.

STEP TWO

1. As your stern clears the bows of Boat A put the rudder over and give a burst ahead to swing your stern round and start coming alongside.

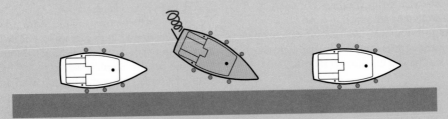

STEP THREE

1. Go astern and bring your boat to a stop.

2. The danger now is dropping back onto Boat A. Pick up your lines and step ashore.

3. Use your stern line as a backspring to prevent your boat dropping back.

4. Make the bow warp fast to stop the bows swinging out.

5. Your boat is now secure and you can continue to put out warps and springs.

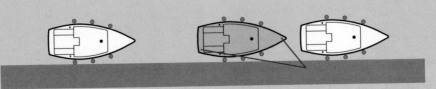

even within the same marina. Try to select a box which is slightly wider and longer than your boat. If you must enter a box significantly wider or longer than your boat there can be problems putting out a second stern line.

Boxes present the single-hander with the dilemma that he should be in the bows ready to step ashore with the lines and at the same time stand in the stern to drop lines round the piles. I have not discovered an arrangement of lines which solves this conundrum.

Entering a Box with a Head Wind

As you enter, loop a line over one pile and secure it with sufficient slack for the bows to just reach the pontoon, letting the wind take the way off your boat. Do not haul on this stern line to take the way off your boat or your bows will swing into the boats on either side. Dash forward and secure the bow lines so that the bows are central in the box. Now loop a second stern line round the other pile, and adjust the lines so that your boat is lying central in the box with the bows clear of the pontoon but close enough for you to climb ashore.

Entering a Box with a Stern Wind

Loop a line over a pile and pay it out as the wind blows you towards the pontoon. Secure when the bows are just short of the pontoon and then proceed as before.

Entering a Box with a Cross Wind

Loop a line over the upwind pile as you enter. Check that it is long enough for the bows to reach the pontoon and secure it. As you lose way there is every chance that your bows will begin to blow off downwind with the possibility of colliding with the downwind boat. Hurry forward, fending off if necessary, step onto the pontoon and secure the upwind bow line. Once this is done then the other lines can be made fast at leisure.

Always double the lines round the piles so that when you come to leave you simply loosen one end and haul it in.

Rafts of yachts alongside on the island of Juist. Note the dinghy, which failed to deter the Botter coming alongside.

RAFTING UP

Try to lie alongside a boat that is the same size as yours or slightly larger. Always give them a hail before going alongside. The crew may be aboard and can help by taking your lines.

Even though they may be rafted up, some outside yachts will leave their dinghies alongside as a hint to go elsewhere. Sometimes skippers will attempt to discourage you from coming alongside by appearing in the hatchway and announcing that they are leaving very early in the morning or in the next half hour, whichever is the soonest. If you have chosen the best (or only) place to berth then be politely ruthless. It is surprising how often these boats change their plans.

If there is no-one aboard the yacht you have chosen to lie against then you must go aboard with your lines. This always involves clambering over guardrails and working on an unfamiliar deck full of tripping hazards. If you are making the bow line fast first, then throwing the stern line into the cockpit as you

Entering a Box Going Ahead

STEP ONE
1. Prepare warps and fenders for berthing in clear water.
2. Check the arrangements for attaching ropes to the piles. On some you simply loop a rope over the pile: others have fixed hooks close to the top of the pile: yet others have sliding arrangements to allow for the tidal range.
3. Approach your berth taking into account the effect of wind and tide.

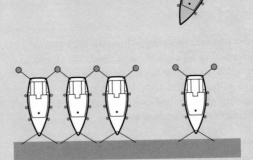

STEP TWO
1. As you enter the berth decide which pile you will loop a rope around.
2. If there is a cross wind or tide then choose the upwind/uptide pile.
3. Prepare the rope to loop round the pile. Check that it will run freely.

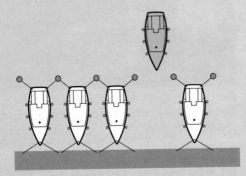

STEP THREE
1. As pile comes abeam the cockpit loop the rope over it.
2. If the wind/tide comes from astern then this is the rope that will hold you off the pontoon. So, let the wind/tide carry you into your berth and at the right moment make the rope fast.
3. Otherwise motor slowly into the berth, stopping before the bows hit the pontoon and then make the rope fast.
4. Go forward to the bows with the bow warp.

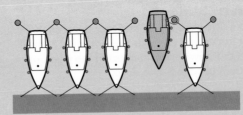

STEP FOUR
1. Step onto the pontoon and make the bow rope fast. Sometimes the easiest way to reach the pontoon is to climb onto a neighbouring boat and over their bows.
2. Make the bow warp fast.
3. Your boat is now secure and you can, at leisure, put a warp out to the second pile and put out a second bow warp.

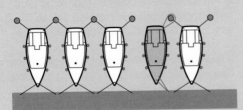

Entering a Box with Restricted Turning Room

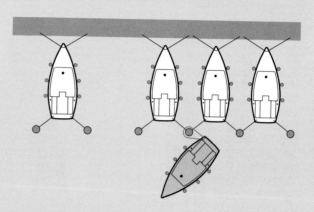

STEP ONE

1. If there is not enough room to turn into your chosen berth then select a downwind, downtide berth.
2. Sail close to a pile opposite, stop engine, and loop a rope around the pile.
3. Pay out the line as the wind and tide swing your boat round.
4. Drop down towards your chosen berth.

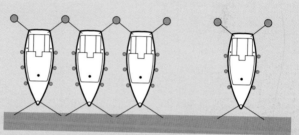

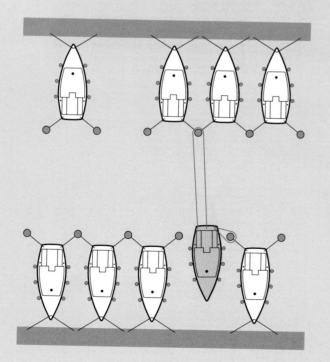

STEP TWO

1. As you enter your chosen berth, loop a line around a pile.
2. Slip your first line.
3. Continue berthing in the usual way.

Entering a Box Going Astern

STEP ONE
1. Not many boats enter boxes astern and if you have a transom-hung rudder, davits or a wind vane, going ashore may be difficult.
2. Entering astern under power requires complete confidence in how your boat handles when going astern.
3. Prepare warps and fenders for berthing in clear water.
4. Approach your berth taking the effects of wind and tide into account.

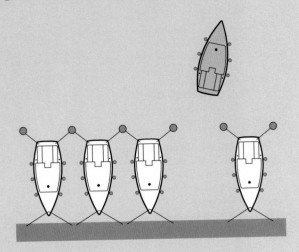

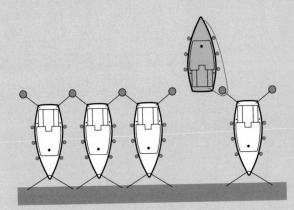

STEP TWO
1. Decide which pile you are going to put your bow warp round. In a cross wind/tide choose the upwind/tide pile.
2. As the pile passes the cockpit loop the bow warp round the pile so that you hold one end and the other runs outside everything to the bows.
3. Pay out this line as you continue to go astern.

STEP THREE
1. Before the stern hits the pontoon make the bow line fast.
2. Step ashore with the stern line and make that fast.
3. Your boat is now secure and you can now tidy up the bow warp, add a line to the other pile and put out a second stern warp.

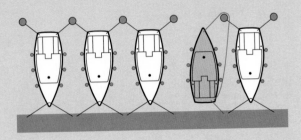

Raft of boats in Funchal Harbour.

come alongside makes good sense, rather than taking it with you to the bows and when you do take it to their stern discover that it is wrapped round their guardrails, fenders and shrouds.

Modern yachts tend to have a few, small mooring cleats. Some yachts tie off their own lines, especially springs, to a perforated metal toe rail. You may need to do the same or use grab rails or winches until you can find empty cleats. Try not to hang onto a stanchion to take the last way off your boat. They have a nasty habit of bending. Springs to the other yacht will prevent you surging back and forth and putting

out shore lines, although not always practicable, is good practice.

Rafts tend to be made up of similar-sized yachts. Some harbours insist on this and paint the harbour wall with boat lengths as a hint. Inevitably there is someone who believes rules are for others and lay their huge gin palace outside you. This always happens when you are ashore. In strong winds there is a real risk of danger to your boat. One option is to offer to lie outside them. If this is refused then you must be politely but completely awkward until they shift.

LOCKS

Some locks have a pontoon inside for yachts to lie to and going alongside that is no different than for any other pontoon. Otherwise, if other boats are going through the lock at the same time as you then the easiest technique is hang back, enter last and raft up to another boat. Once your lines are secure to the other boat you have nothing to do but wait for the lock to fill (or empty). When the gates open you will be one of the first out.

If you must lie to the lock wall then enter as slowly as possible and check out the mooring points. This is one of the rare occasions when it is impossible to carry out a reconnaissance before committing yourself to a manoeuvre. Locks usually have ladders set in the wall. In addition some have rows of small bollards set in small alcoves in the wall and some have ropes strung along the wall for crews to hold onto without using mooring lines. A few allow you to step ashore and double your lines round bollards. Never make lines fast either to bollards or to your boat or you may find your boat hanging from its cleats. Locks tend to be tide and current free but sometimes there is a movement of water in or out of the lock. Check the wind direction as you enter and if possible berth to windward so that when you come to leave the lock you are blown off the lock wall, otherwise you may need to spring off.

The problem for the single-hander is that it is almost impossible lie to doubled bow and stern lines in a lock. The space between bollards is normally greater than the length of your boat so that after hooking a stern line over a bollard, you must carry your way to the next bollard while you dash forward to the bows to secure the bow line. However, the slightest snagging of the stern line will cause the bows to swing out and instantly you are broadside in the lock with the danger of hitting other boats. From bitter experience I know it is very difficult to bring the bows back in. Unless you can guarantee reaching the bow bollard in time do not even try.

Hooking both bow and stern lines over the same bollard, standing midships and controlling them from there can be successful but there is always the risk of the bow or stern swinging slightly out as the lock fills or empties. The best solution I have found is to take advantage of the fact that ladders are normally about halfway between two bollards. I come alongside so that the stern is opposite a bollard and drop a stern line round it. I then go midships to the ladder taking the stern line with me and put a bight of the midships line round the ladder. Standing midships or slightly forward of midships it is a simple matter to change the rung the midship line is round as the lock fills or empties. It is very difficult to change the stern line to a new bollard. Provided the line is long enough this is no problem in an emptying lock for the pull is always downwards and the line remains secure. In a filling lock the bollard can disappear under water and the pull is upwards, with the risk of the stern line slipping off. The only answer I have found is not to haul hard on the stern line.

Berthing to a Ladder

If there are no bollards or a line to hang onto then you will have to put both lines round a rung in the ladder. As you approach the ladder, go midships carrying the stern line and take a bight round a rung. Do the same with the midships line. Stand midships or slightly forward of midships and control the lines as the lock fills or empties and change rungs accordingly. Like berthing to a ladder or single bollard, it can be difficult to keep your boat lying quietly to the wall, but it will be impossible for your boat to swing broadside and with any reasonable luck there will nothing more than the occasional oscillation.

Berthing to a Rope on the Lock Wall

The ropes strung along a lock wall are normally attached to eyebolts spaced along the wall. As you reach one eyebolt pass the stern line through the rope so that it cannot slip forward of the eyebolt. Holding the

Entering and berthing in a busy lock is a time for quick decisions, it is important to have warps and fenders ready and expect that as you go alongside one boat another will be berthing alongside you. As it is easier to hang onto another boat than the wall try not to be amongst the first boats into the lock.

stern line, go midships or slightly forward of midships and hold on to the rope strung along the lock wall.

If you are lying to a wall in a lock you must be anti-social and discourage anyone from rafting up to you. You will have enough problems controlling your own boat. For this reason, if there are a number of boats waiting to enter a lock wait, until at least some of them have secured themselves to the wall and then raft up to another boat.

PICKING UP A BUOY

When you come to pick up a buoy there is rarely any problem in coming up to it and stopping. The problem is that between leaving the cockpit and reaching the bows to pick up the buoy, wind and tide can have carried you away and you cannot reach it with a line. There are patented boathooks with automatic line fastening devices, which

will extend your reach, but even these may not be long enough.

Catching the buoy with a boathook and making fast while holding onto the boathook is done more to entertain onlookers than actually making fast to the buoy.

One solution is to have a loop of line with a shackle attached to its centre and bring the buoy alongside the cockpit and cast a loop of line over the buoy. The shackle encourages the line to sink, and when it is under the buoy it will snag the buoy's riser. Holding onto the looped line, go to the bows and bring the buoy and its line aboard in the usual way.

If you have to make fast directly to the buoy then rig a line from the bows going outside everything and bring this back to the cockpit. Snag the buoy with the

Picking up a buoy

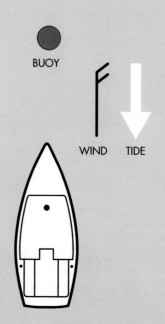

BUOY

WIND   TIDE

STEP ONE
1. If the short-handed sailor brings the buoy up to his bows then by the time he has moved from the cockpit to the bows wind and tide will have carried the buoy out of reach.
2. One solution is:
(a) have a length of line in hand in the cockpit.
(b) sail or motor up to the buoy a couple of times, stop and establish your direction and rate of drift.
3. Then approach the buoy with the intention of bringing it alongside the cockpit.

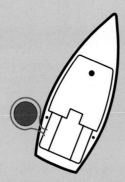

STEP TWO
1. When alongside the buoy pick up the length of line and holding it in both hands throw the loop over the buoy.
2. Let the line sink. A shackle on the line may help.
3. Pull the line in so as to catch the buoys riser.
4. Your boat is now attached to the buoy.

STEP THREE
1. Keeping a hold of the line lead the buoy to the bows and make both ends of the line fast. You now have a temporary mooring.
2. As appropriate you can now:
(a) Make your own mooring line fast.
(b) Bring the buoy aboard and use its mooring line.
(c) If mooring between two buoys pick up the bridle between the buoys, drop back, pick up the second buoy and then adjust the mooring lines as necessary.

Caribbean Anchorage.

weighted line as before and make both ends of the loop fast. Next, attach the line from the bows to the buoy. Cast off the loop and let the boat drop back on the wind and tide, and once the buoy has reached the bows adjust the line so that you are lying comfortably. If lying between two buoys it is usual to pick up the bow buoy first. Beware of the propeller fouling the bridle between the buoys as you approach. Make fast at the bows as already described and then, using the bridle as a guide, drop back to pick up the stern buoy. Holding the bridle will help keep you in line if the tide is swinging you across the buoys.

ANCHORING

Before entering an anchorage check state of the tide and calculate amount of line or chain required. In calm waters, away from other boats, flake the required amount of line or chain out on deck. Make sure it will run easily. Trusting line or chain to run out of hawse pipe carries the risk of it kinking and jamming in the hawse pipe but if you are certain that this will not happen and your line or chain is clearly marked so you know how much is out, then you can omit this step. When you enter an anchorage first look for a spot to anchor. In busy anchorages, areas free of anchored boats often conceal hazards

The Working Anchor

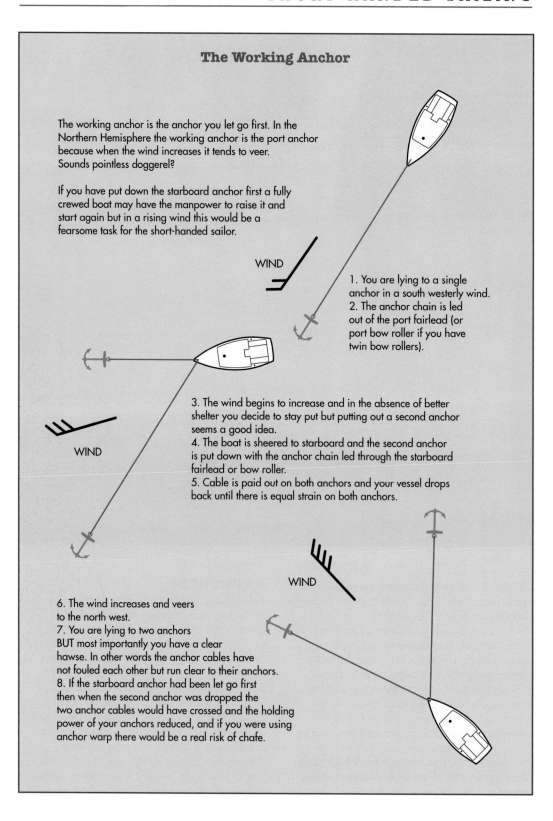

The working anchor is the anchor you let go first. In the Northern Hemisphere the working anchor is the port anchor because when the wind increases it tends to veer.
Sounds pointless doggerel?

If you have put down the starboard anchor first a fully crewed boat may have the manpower to raise it and start again but in a rising wind this would be a fearsome task for the short-handed sailor.

WIND

1. You are lying to a single anchor in a south westerly wind.
2. The anchor chain is led out of the port fairlead (or port bow roller if you have twin bow rollers).

3. The wind begins to increase and in the absence of better shelter you decide to stay put but putting out a second anchor seems a good idea.
4. The boat is sheered to starboard and the second anchor is put down with the anchor chain led through the starboard fairlead or bow roller.
5. Cable is paid out on both anchors and your vessel drops back until there is equal strain on both anchors.

WIND

WIND

6. The wind increases and veers to the north west.
7. You are lying to two anchors BUT most importantly you have a clear hawse. In other words the anchor cables have not fouled each other but run clear to their anchors.
8. If the starboard anchor had been let go first then when the second anchor was dropped the two anchor cables would have crossed and the holding power of your anchors reduced, and if you were using anchor warp there would be a real risk of chafe.

Entering Anchorage

STEP ONE
1. Read pilot and sailing directions.
2. Check depth of water, tides and range of tide.
3. In clear water outside of anchorage:
(a) have anchor ready to go
(b) flake out enough chain on deck
(c) have a line to hand in case you have to pick
up buoy or take a line ashore.
4. If entering under sail then reduce sail to the
minimum necessary to enter anchorage. Check
that the sails are ready to be lowered and sail ties handy.
5. Enter anchorage check how other boats are lying.
6. Select where you will drop your anchor (X) and
where your boat will be when the chain is out (Y).

X

Y

STEP TWO
1. Sail up to Point X.
2. Lower anchor until it is up and down.
3. Pay out the chain as your boat drops back.

X

Y

STEP THREE
1. All your prepared cable should be out
when you reach Point Y.
2. If you have not prepared enough cable then let
out more until you are at Point Y. (Cunning short-handed
sailors sail over Point Y when checking out the anchorage
and note a couple of cross transits on shore. This allows
them to check their position while working in the bows.)
3. When satisfied the anchor is holding and you are clear
of other boats then stop engine (or stow sails) and take
anchor bearings for the log.

English Harbour, Antigua.

such as rocks, cables or foul ground. If you think there is any risk of the anchor fouling, then fit a tripping line.

If anchoring astern of another vessel:

- go close to its stern. This boat will be lying to the wind and tide and its attitude is a good indicator of how you will lie;
- lower the anchor;
- when it reaches the bottom and bites then drop back on the wind and tide, paying out line or chain as you go;
- when line or chain is all out, check the anchor is holding by bearings and transit;
- holding can be improved by putting the engine astern for a moment or two once all the line or chain is out . If you do not drag, the anchor is holding;
- take final anchor bearings and enter them in the log...remember you may need to check these at night so select features that can be used day or night.

If you are anchoring near another vessel, make sure that you are far enough apart so that your turning circles will not bring you together.

Unless I am sure that I can dive on the anchor and check how it lies, then I prefer fitting a tripping line. For me, donning a mask and fins and inspecting the anchor is confined to warm tropical waters but there is no doubt that it is the surest way of confirming that the anchor is set properly and will be recovered easily. If the anchor needs to be reset then it is surprisingly easy to pick it up and move it to a better location.

If you are anchoring in an empty featureless anchorage, a coral cay for example, it is often difficult to find enough features for anchor bearings. Go out in the dinghy, and clear of your own anchor line, drop an anchor buoy (a fender will do) on a line just longer than the calculated maximum depth. Note the position of this buoy relative to the boat. This is a help in deciding if you have dragged and an independent back up to the GPS anchor alarm.

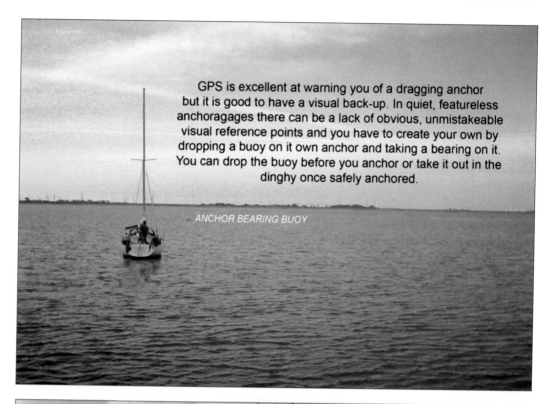

GPS is excellent at warning you of a dragging anchor
but it is good to have a visual back-up. In quiet, featureless
anchoragages there can be a lack of obvious, unmistakeable
visual reference points and you have to create your own by
dropping a buoy on it own anchor and taking a bearing on it.
You can drop the buoy before you anchor or take it out in the
dinghy once safely anchored.

ANCHOR BEARING BUOY

Anchorage on Rio Macareo.

9 Passage Planning

One of sailing's few certainties is that the greatest errors occur when you assume the truth and accuracy of information you have not personally verified before setting out. Perhaps the means of checking may not be available, or at least not in a form you understand. Foreign language sailing directions come into this category. Or, you may be sailing on old, uncorrected charts. No one admits to this but we all do. Probably the most common sin is that you have made the passage before, assume that you possess total recall and that nothing has changed since your last visit.

Planning to transit the Caledonian Canal we sailed up Loch Linnhe intending to anchor opposite Fort William's railway station. Although it was night I knew the area well and was completely confident about anchoring opposite the unlit railway station pier, which was convenient to a local hostelry. How I was to know that they had moved the railway station? And built a by-pass along the shore? Waiting for the traffic on the main road to disappear into the town it needed one of the crew to remind me that we were a long way up the loch.

Every passage, however short, however familiar, should be planned as though you are making it for the first time. This holds true for everyone but especially the short-handed sailor. At sea he must be able to accept the information in his passage plan as complete and accurate without question, for he has not the time to start checking the information in it from scratch.

DEFINING THE PASSAGE PLAN

A passage plan is not a programme describing events that, mechanically followed, will bring you to your destination, but a collection of information on sailing from A to B that allows you to respond intelligently to the unexpected the actual voyage throws up. No plan, however carefully written, works. When Plan A goes awry the short-handed sailor cannot start consulting pilots and charts to prepare Plan B. If he does then Plan B will be put together hurriedly, in the dark, dripping water over the chart table on a boat that is being thrown casually from wave to wave in the middle of a busy shipping lane. The probability of his revised plan containing errors and misjudgements is very high. It is far better to put too much information in your original passage plan and ignore 90% of it, than to be short of that one item of vital information when you really need it.

Examining variations and alternatives to your preferred route before you sail means that your passage plan is written at leisure. It is possible to gather and assess information from a wide range of sources including reference books, the Internet, and from those sailors who have recently made the same or similar passages. You will never cover every eventuality but you should put enough information in your passage plan to make an intelligent response to unexpected events.

DEPARTURE AND LANDFALL

Pilotage

Every voyage begins and ends with piloting your boat in or out of harbour. Pilotage is interactive nautical map reading using terrestrial features and sea marks to determine your position and confirm your course. Strong currents or eddies may mean having to helm rather than using the autohelm, and the movement of other vessels can lead to unexpected changes of course or speed. The short-handed sailor is busy with several tasks at once and the risk of distraction and subsequent disorientation is high. A typical example is staring ahead desperately searching for the next

PASSAGE PLANNING CHECKLIST

DATE	Time Zone		Sunrise		Sunset	
FROM	Latitude				Longitude	
TO	Latitude				Longitude	
DISTANCE	ETD		ETA		ETE	

TIDES

Date	Name	HW 1	HW 2	LW 1	LW 2
Standard Port 1					
Secondary Port 1					
Differences					
Times					
Standard Port 2					
Secondary Port 2					
Differences					
Times					

TIDAL STREAMS

Time	North		South		East		West	
	Set		Set		Set		Set	
		Drift		Drift		Drift		Drift
Mean Tidal Set			Current Set					
Mean Tidal Drift			Current Drift					

LIMITATIONS TO TIMINGS

	Factor	Time
Tidal Harbours...departure		
Tidal Harbour...arrival		
Tidal Gates...eg Alderney Race		
Daylight Departure		
Daylight Arrival		
Lock opening times		
Bridge opening times		

CHARTS

	Title	Number	Folio

PILOTS

	Title	Page(s)

WEATHER

Latest forecast before departure	Time of Origin

Forecasts

Source	Frequency/VHF	Times

LIGHTS

	Light	Latitude	Longitude	Characteristic	Range	ETOS

DAYMARKS

	Mark	Latitude	Longitude	Description	ETOS

HAZARDS

Hazard	Description	Latitude	Longitude	Clearing Brg	Clearing Wpt
Rocks					
Shoals					
Overfalls					
TSS					
Oil/gas Rigs					
Other					

COMMUNICATIONS

Organisation	Callsign	Frequency	Times
Coastguard			
Port Working Channel 1			
Port Working Channel 2			
Locks			
Bridges			
Other			

LIMITATIONS TO LEAVING HARBOUR

Wind	Sea State	Visiblity

PORTS OF REFUGE

Port	Latitude	Longitude	Landfall Latitude	Landfall Longitude	Chart	Pilot

ROUTEING

Pilotage Out Of Harbour

From	To	Course (C)	Distance	ETE	Remarks
Berth/Anchorage					
	Point of Departure				

Passage Making

From	To	Course (C)	Distance	ETE	Remarks
	Point of Departure				
Landfall					

Pilotage Into Harbour

From	To	Course (C)	Distance	ETE	Remarks
Landfall					
	Berth/Anchorage				

buoy and missing the very large container ship coming up astern. It is not a time to be down below reading the chart or to be consulting the pilot.

It helps to know your course relative to some prominent, unmistakable feature. The sun is good, so too are conspicuous landmarks, and there is also the compass, or even better, all three. Then, whatever the distraction, this makes checking your position and heading after carrying out some other task is quick and simple.

Study the charts and pilots beforehand and identify the prominent features that you expect to see and the order in which you reckon to pick them up. Prominent is relative. A 20-metre high light on Scotland's mountainous west coast is unlikely to leap to the eye but on the low lying Dutch coast it will dominate the landscape for miles. Be aware of features of similar appearance. On the Elbe between the sea and Cuxhaven are the wooden beacons of Neuwerk North, Neuwerk South and the Kugel Bake. They all have a strong family resemblance. Mistaking one for the other is easily done and could be extremely embarrassing.

Although pilotage is almost entirely navigating by eye, entering carefully selected waypoints into the GPS helps. Imagine that you have reached a junction of three or four channels. The first buoy in each channel is some distance off; which is the correct buoy?

On the chart the answer is obvious, but on a featureless seascape less so. For a variety of reasons you may distrust the bearing you have written down. You may not believe the compass. You may convince yourself that the channel has shifted and the buoy moved. We are genetically programmed to make what we see fit what we expect to see. This is at its most apparent when making a landfall or in busy channels. The GPS independently confirms your noted distance and bearing to the next buoy, and a check with the handbearing compass will nearly always bring it into view.

Be wary of any assumptions about what you expect to see. Entering Dunmore East for the first time on a wet and windy night I assumed that Hook Light (46 metres ASL) was, like St Catherine's Light (41 metres ASL) on the Isle of Wight, on top of the cliffs fringing Ireland's south coast. My plan was to round the headland, pick up the harbour lights and steer for the yacht club bar. Long before I reached the headland the harbour lights became visible when they should have been obscured by the cliffs. How was I to know that Hook Light is not a low lighthouse on a cliff but a very tall lighthouse on a low spit of land with the harbour, and its lights, in clear view beyond? The answer, of course, is that I should have read the pilot before I set sail, not after I reached harbour. For the curious, Hook Light is 35 metres (115 feet) tall and St Catherine's is 27 metres (88.5 feet).

Night Pilotage.

Night-time pilotage can be both simpler and more challenging than during the day. The classic time for landfall is to arrive just before dawn and enter harbour with the sun rising astern, but there are many occasions when you arrive in the dark, small hours.

Pilotage in the dark is straightforward provided there is a solitary short channel with a handful of lights. It is extremely demanding if there is a network of long channels with a heavy concentration of cardinal and lateral lights, multiple leading lights, anchored ships and entire constellations of shore lights. What appears obvious on the chart can be very confusing in reality.

Darkness destroys perspective. Doubts abound. Are you looking at a distant, bright light or a nearby dim light that you are about to hit? When you are timing a light, sometimes other lights on nearly the same bearing can confuse matters so much that with only a hint of wishful thinking any light can have any characteristic you desire. Shadows look like solid breakwaters and breakwaters, rocks and even anchored ships look like open sea. Car headlights and brake lights rounding a corner can take on the characteristics of a buoy or a shorelight.

Taking buoys one at a time is good advice in daytime and an absolute rule at night. Prepare a list of the buoys you will pass together with their characteristics, and the bearing, distance and estimated time en route between one buoy and the next. If you prefer, the positions of the buoys can be entered into the GPS as waypoints and then the GPS will produce this information automatically. Some work directly on the chart but I like the information on paper. This allows me to write down the time I pass each buoy. If I am distracted it is the work of an instant to check where I am and where I am going. If you reach a buoy before the next is positively identified then slow down as you approach it. Nearly always the next buoy, and sometimes the one after, appears as you approach. If not, then heave-to or circle the buoy and look down the bearing to the next buoy. Binoculars can help, but only if the sea is relatively calm. In anything of a sea, lights become wandering streaks when seen through binoculars. Only continue when the next buoy is confidently identified. The short-handed sailor can only do one task at a time. It is far safer to stop the boat in safe water until the next buoy is identified rather than continue sailing still looking for the buoy.

Preserving night vision is another reason I prefer making notes to using the chart. It takes about twenty minutes for full night vision to build up and a couple of microseconds to lose it by switching on a white light. A short-handed sailor cannot afford to be blinded every time he looks at the chart. It is possible to read large black print on a white back-ground in most lights, even star light. If you must have light, then red lights are kinder to night vision than white but reading a chart by red light is extremely difficult.

Few torches come with built in colour filters. Depending on how red you wish the light to be, try taping one or two layers of red acetate over the lens on a torch. Some like painting red nail varnish over the lens but this gives an uneven colour. If you want a low power red light that you can hang up on the pramhood and run from the ship's batteries, then make your own LED lamp. LEDs have a life of several thousand hours, draw almost no current, are no drain on the battery and can be left on all night.

Local knowledge allows you to enter harbours in conditions that are unsafe for a visitor. Local knowledge means that you are up to date on all the latest changes, even those that have not yet reached the pilot book or chart makers; the lights are familiar friends; you know the quirks of the tide, the shortcuts to take and the corners to cut. Strangers, by definition, lack this information although discussing your plans with local yachtsmen and listening to their advice can help bridge the gap. If cruising abroad then charts and pencil sketches are a great help in making good the lack of a common language when quizzing sailors about their local harbours.

Day or night, keen eyesight is a prime requirement for safe pilotage and a pair of good binoculars, preferably with a built-in compass, is useful in to confirm the shape and colour of a buoy, in helping to pick out a line of buoys and, if they are very good, in helping to clarify the picture at night.

When you are sailing down a channel it is easy to become obsessed by the buoys you will pass, but there are features outside the channel that are useful. These include prominent buildings, hills, radio masts and beacons. At night there will be lights outside the channel winking away insisting on being identified, and including their details on the pilotage pro forma means that when you do pick them up they can be quickly identified.

EN ROUTE
En route covers the period between leaving your point of departure and arriving at your landfall. Navigation is primarily concerned with finding and keeping to the quickest route to your destination, taking into account the effect of wind, tides, weather and currents. These may change several times in the course of a passage and your final route may have little resemblance to your original plan. The en route phase may last several hours or weeks.

HARBOURS OF REFUGE

A harbour of refuge is a harbour, marina or anchorage that you may divert to because of

a. stress of weather, which can take the form of too much wind, headwinds, not enough wind, poor visibility or some combination of these factors.
b. some gear failure which has so reduced boat performance that to continue with repairs would be foolhardy.
c. a medical emergency

A harbour of refuge can be entered safely in any weather at any stage of the tide. It should not have a bar and its approach should be free of off-lying hazards. If there are any hazards then they should all be unmistakably marked. Its entrance should be obvious by day or by night. Once in harbour there should be enough room for you to round up and prepare fenders and warps for berthing.

If there are any limitations, such as it can only be entered so many hours either side of high water, or if there are any objective dangers, such as off-lying shoals or rocks, highlight these in you passage plan.

DANGERS

Dangers that you meet en route include features such as rocks, shoals, tide races and tidal overfalls. Some have varying levels of danger. On a calm day it may be possible to sail over a shoal that in a gale is a confusion of hungry, ship-eating seas. In heavy winds you cheerfully accept the extra miles from leaving a shoal to windward when the shortest route leaves it to leeward. Taking the inside passage to the Portland Race on a quiet day is a good example of a hazard given a very wide berth in heavy weather. A well-marked isolated rock may be a splendid means of confirming your position on a fine day and a deadly hazard in poor visibility.

All dangers should be identified and a course laid using waypoints, which will keep you well clear. Depending on actual conditions you may decide to cut corners but at the planning stage you assume the worst. Cutting the corners can be included amongst your

options, and the decision on whether or not they are taken up made en route when the actual, rather than forecast, conditions can be taken into account.

LIGHTS

All lights that you expect to pick up along your intended route should be identified and noted on your passage plan together with the time and bearing you expect to see them. It is best to base your estimate on the time you will physically see the light and accept that in some conditions you will pick up its loom long before you see the actual light. Do this even if you expect to pass every light in bright sunshine. If you are delayed you do not wish to add to your problems by wondering, 'What is that light over there?'

Even in this age of electronic navigation, lights still provide a satisfying way of checking your position and confirming progress over the ground. The time you expect to pick up the light will be updated to reflect your actual performance, but if it is not picked up within a few minutes of your latest estimate then it is prudent to check your position.

TIDES

You must know:

● the times of high and low water for your departure point, destination and harbours of refuge.
● if any are drying harbours note the times when there will enough water for you to enter.
● if you are on springs or neaps.
● areas like the Alderney Race which can only be traversed with a favourable tide.
● the direction and rate of tidal stream you expect to meet on passage.

This information can be obtained in the traditional way from the tide tables, tidal atlas and the tidal diamonds on the chart or from specialist computer programmes.

With tides do not become obsessed with the figures on the right of the decimal point. Always keep the broad picture in mind. Wind over tide usually carries a health warning, and avoid areas of fierce tides when strong winds

SOURCES OF WEATHER FORECASTS

1. Newspapers: Even foreign newspapers print weather forecasts in understandable pictorial form.

2. Radio: Apart from the BBC Shipping Forecast local radio stations in coastal areas often include weather forecasts for leisure sailors. There are private radio stations like Herb for the North Atlantic and DP07 for the German coasts which broadcast forecasts tailored for yachtsmen. You learn about these stations from the grapevine in your sailing area. Unless you speak the local language fluently or they broadcast in English, like the Dutch Coastguard, it pays to learn the local terms for gale warnings, wind speeds and direction and listen very carefully.

3. TV: All television stations broadcast regular weather forecasts. They are mostly concerned with weather over land but are better than nothing. Services like Teletext broadcast shipping forecasts.

4. Internet: Just now this is really an onshore option but that is likely to change as technology improves. The Internet is full of weather sites. Use a search engine like Google and type in 'weather forecast' and take your pick. The Internet allows you to compare forecasts from different national weather agencies. If you are sailing around the Channel Islands or planning a Biscay crossing you can compare the UK Met Office forecast with Meteo France. National weather agencies tend to be at their best around their coasts. The UK Met Office treats Biscay as a single sea area while Meteo France divides it into four.

5. Navtex: The international Navtex broadcasts are in English. The national Navtex broadcasts are in the local language.

6. Wefax: To receive a weather fax you need either a dedicated Wefax receiver or a SSB receiver, demodulator, laptop and weatherfax programme such as JVFax. JVFax is a shareware programme and can be downloaded from the Internet. You also need the frequencies and times of the weatherfax broadcasts for your area. Weatherfaxes can be received onshore or at sea.

7. Local coastguard: Most coastguard services broadcast inshore weather forecasts and issue strong wind warnings. Abroad these are usually in the local language.

8. Harbour authorities: Port authorities and marinas often display the local forecast.

blow over the tide. The Elbe, for example, is effectively closed to yachts when there is much more than a force five blowing over the ebb. Similarly there are overfalls off many headlands that must be given a very wide berth in heavy weather. In shallow water the wind can significantly raise or lower the predicted tidal heights. A westerly wind on the Dutch coast brings higher than expected tides, an easterly lower than predicted.

WEATHER AND WEATHER FORECASTS

Start collecting weather forecasts several days before you intend to sail. This builds up an understanding of the current weather pattern, which helps you to evaluate the forecast when you come to depart. If possible compare forecasts from different sources. Often they are variations on a common theme, and how close these variations are to each other is a good measure of forecast accuracy. Assume the forecast giving the worst weather is right.

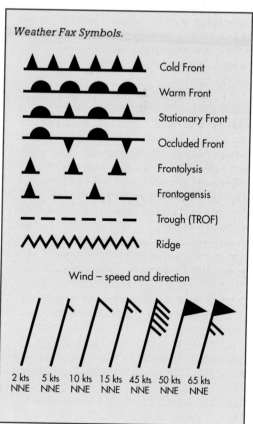

Weather Fax Symbols.

Cold Front
Warm Front
Stationary Front
Occluded Front
Frontolysis
Frontogensis
Trough (TROF)
Ridge

Wind – speed and direction

| 2 kts | 5 kts | 10 kts | 15 kts | 45 kts | 50 kts | 65 kts |
| NNE | NNE | NNE | NNE | NNE | NNE | NNE |

The days when just about the only source of weather forecasts for yachtsmen was the BBC shipping forecast have long gone. Nowadays weather forecasts can be obtained from many different sources and there is so much weather information available that it is always possible to obtain an up-to-date forecast for your sea area before sailing, and to know the broad weather picture and how it has developed over the last few days. Synoptic charts are good for the general picture and a collection of these built up over a period of days helps bridge gaps in your forecasts for the first few days at sea.

PILOT/ROUTEING CHARTS

Pilot or routeing charts are not weather forecasts. They contain information month by month, one chart per month, on the average winds and seas for every 5 degree box in the major oceans of the world. They have two drawbacks. First, collecting data requires reporting stations. Historically many of these have been ships on passage so that the information is most complete and the figures most accurate on well-travelled ocean routes. If you intend to sail deep in the Southern Ocean, data on routeing charts may be sparse.

Secondly, pilot charts deal in averages which can conceal extremes but they give you a good idea of the weather you expect to meet, and by using the information on winds and currents you can calculate your boat's likely performance 5 degree box by 5 degree box along your chosen route and any selected variations that catch your eye. If you are planning a long passage then long before you cast off dry sailing can pass many a winter's evening and help you build up a good idea of what you can expect to meet.

Dry sailing is much more than comparing distances over the ground. Knowing the likely wind speed and direction allows you to vary your estimated boat speed depending on whether you are close hauled, close reaching, broad reaching or running.

Estimates of your boat's performance on various points of sail are based on your knowledge of your boat. As a cross check against your time for the overall route try using half your maximum hull speed as found from $1.3\sqrt{LWL}/2$ and dividing the answer into the rumb line or great circle distance to obtain your expected time on passage. It appears rough and ready but it gives a surprisingly accurate estimate of the passage time for cruising boats. The actual weather you encounter may bear little relationship to the pilot chart, but with the information gleaned from your armchair sailing you are well placed to react positively to the actual weather conditions you encounter.

Using the information on the wind and current roses, calculating likely weather and boat performance is time consuming and the calculations for a long passage and its possible variations can take several days. Nowadays there are computer programmes that will carry out this task at the press of a button or two, and allow you to quickly compare routes and different times of year.

For example, according to tradition, square riggers sailing from Falmouth to La Coruña headed west until the Pole Star was on their backstay before sailing south. Presumably this reduced the risk of being embayed in Biscay. Dry sailing this route shows that they preferred beating over 100 nautical miles from Start Point through the Western Approaches. They also accepted a huge time penalty. This route is 520 nautical miles compared to 435 nautical miles taking the rhumb line route from Start Point.

Not only does the rhumb line route avoid thrashing to windward but once the bows are pointed at La Coruña the route goes through a different wind pattern with the winds more westerly than the south-west winds of the traditional route. Perhaps the old timers worried over a gale pushing them into Biscay but in June and July the chance of a gale is around 1% and calms between 5-6%. The expected winds are around Beaufort Force 3/4. The greatest drawback to the rhumb line route is that it goes very close to the traffic separation scheme off Ushant.

SPEED CONVERSION TABLE

KNOTS	MPH	KPH	BEAUFORT	DESCRIPTION
1	1.2	1.9	1	Light Air
2	2.3	3.7	1	
3	3.5	5.6	1	
4	4.6	7.4	2	Light Breeze
5	5.8	9.3	2	
6	6.9	11.1	2	
7	8.1	13.0	3	Gentle Breeze
8	9.2	14.8	3	
9	10.4	16.7	3	
10	11.5	18.5	3	
11	12.7	20.4	4	Moderate Breeze
12	13.8	22.2	4	
13	15.0	24.1	4	
14	16.1	25.9	4	
15	17.3	27.8	4	
16	18.4	29.6	5	Fresh Breeze
17	19.6	31.5	5	
18	20.7	33.3	5	
19	21.9	35.2	5	
20	23.0	37.0	5	
21	24.2	38.9	6	Strong Breeze
22	25.3	40.7	6	
23	26.5	42.6	6	
24	27.6	44.4	6	
25	28.8	46.3	6	
26	29.9	48.2	6	
27	31.1	50.0	7	Moderate Gale
28	32.2	51.9	7	
29	33.4	53.7	7	
30	34.5	55.6	7	
31	35.7	57.4	7	
32	36.8	59.3	7	
33	38.0	61.1	8	Fresh Gale
34	39.1	63.0	8	
35	40.3	64.8	8	
36	41.4	66.7	8	
37	42.6	68.5	8	
38	43.7	70.4	8	
39	44.9	72.2	8	
40	46.0	74.1	8	
41	47.2	75.9	9	Strong Gale
42	48.3	77.8	9	
43	49.5	79.6	9	
44	50.6	81.5	9	
45	51.8	83.3	9	
46	52.9	85.2	9	
47	54.1	87.0	9	
48	55.2	88.9	10	Whole Gale
49	56.4	90.7	10	
50	57.5	92.6	10	

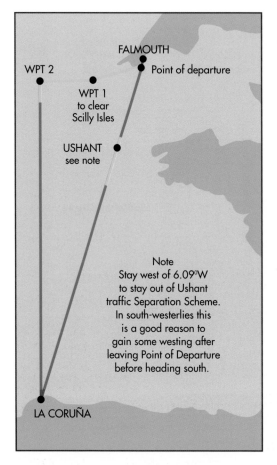

FALMOUTH

WPT 2

Point of departure

WPT 1
to clear
Scilly Isles

USHANT
see note

Note
Stay west of 6.09°W
to stay out of Ushant
traffic Separation Scheme.
In south-westerlies this
is a good reason to
gain some westing after
leaving Point of Departure
before heading south.

LA CORUÑA

FALMOUTH TO LA CORUÑA DRY SAILING COMPARISION		
Heading	**Route 1**	**Route 2**
Rhumb line Distance	522nm	435nm
Estimated Time En Route	6.5 days	4.2 days
Average Boat Speed	3.4 knots	4.3 Knots
Distance spent beating	115nm	0
Distance close reaching	92nm	62nm
Average Wind Direction	300°T	310°T
Average Wind Speed	12 knots	11 knots
Average Current Set	152°T	172°T
Average Current Drift	0.5 knots	0.5 knots
Average Wave Height	4.3 feet	4.1 feet

Route 1 is the traditional square rigger route of sailing west until La Coruña bears south. Route 2 is the direct rhumbline route.

Dry sailing boat routes shows that not only is the traditional longer but that almost 40% of the time is spent either beating or close reaching.

By comparison, the direct route has no beating and less than 10% of the distance is spent close reaching.

Another option is to make for the Channel Islands and sail round the coast. This transforms the crossing into a series of long day passages and, provided you were always prepared to wait for good weather, free of the risk of being caught in a gale in Biscay. At over 880 nautical miles and with between 15-20 overnight stops it would take much longer.

Limitations Imposed by Weather

An important element of passage planning is deciding the weather conditions in which you will not leave harbour. These may be conditions that keep everyone in port. Or it may be weather you prefer not to sail in. For example, you may decide not to sail in headwinds of force five or above, or if the forecast visibility is poor. The exact conditions you choose not to sail in are a mixture of

1. personal preferences
2. your vessel's performance
3. the abilities and experience of your crew or lack of crew.

It is easier to stick to your limitations if you decide on them at the planning stage rather than waiting until you are ready to sail, when the pressures to put to sea can become

Fresh Rations for Trans-Atlantic Passage: a fridge or even a freezer is useful for keeping food fresh longer but fresh food and vegetables keep well provided they are hung in nets and checked every day.

irresistible. As a rule the short-handed sailor will remain tucked up in harbour in conditions welcomed by hard-nosed racing crews.

It is also wise, before you sail, to lay down the weather conditions, forecast or actual, that may be met en route that will cause you to divert to a port of refuge. In the event you may well decide not to divert, but at least this

is a positive decision rather than simply carrying on because you cannot think of anything better.

COMMUNICATIONS

Many of the decisions you make en route will be based on updating your original information, and you need to know the radio services which provide some of these updates. Note down

a. the times, channels and frequencies for weather forecasts. These may be from coastguards, weatherfax or some other source.
b. the coastguard working frequencies.
c. port working channels for your destination and ports of refuge: some ports, for example Dover, Ramsgate and Lowestoft require all craft to radio ahead for permission to enter.
d. the channels used by any traffic control schemes you are likely to encounter.

I often just miss a broadcast I was sure of catching and I have taken to setting the egg timer to remind me to tune in.

CHARTS

Make a list of the charts you will use and the order in which you will use them. Then store them in that order, folded if necessary so that the area of the chart you will first use is immediately obvious. As you sail off one chart, put it to the bottom of the pile and take the next from the top. Stowed like this the next chart you use is always the chart on top.

RATIONS

For a day sail or even an overnight passage you can subsist on ready made sandwiches and flasks of soup and coffee. For longer sails you must carry sufficient rations and water plus a surplus for your passage. How large a surplus is a matter of judgement, but another useful rule of thumb is to victual for the expected time on passage, plus an additional 50%. For a four-day passage carry rations for six days.

What constitutes a day's rations depends on your preferences and whether or not you have a fridge or freezer to extend the life of fresh food. I calculate a day's rations on eating breakfast, a snack lunch, a decent evening meal plus a selection of snacks and hot drinks as treats between meals. If you are making a blue water passage and lack fridge or freezer, then after the first couple of weeks menus tend to be dominated by dried and canned food, pasta and pulses. The water ration is one gallon per person per day for the expected time en route plus 50%.

I also carry heavy-weather rations of tempting but sustaining goodies that can be eaten either with no preparation or very little preparation.

STOWAGE
Before setting out, the boat must be properly stowed. If you have been living aboard in harbour or at anchor, the cabin may look like the parlour of a country cottage. Before you sail everything must be properly stowed for sea.

SLEEPING ARRANGEMENTS
At sea everyone must have a bunk of their own where lee cloths or boards allow them to sleep comfortably regardless of weather. Avoid the temptation of hot bunking. Hot bunking is only an option on short passages of up to about thirty hours or so. Longer, and it is better for everyone to have their own bunk, and on blue water passages this becomes essential for there will be times when it is best, and safest, for everyone to be in their bunk.

MEDICAL
At least one person aboard should have a first aid certificate. Always check the contents of the medical box and the ready-to-use medical bag, and make sure they are complete and up to date.

Find out if anyone aboard is on medication or if they suffer from any condition which means they should stay ashore. If you are sailing with your family you probably know the answers to these questions but friends sometimes surprise you. If you are in doubt ask them to check with their doctor before sailing.

If you are sailing in European waters everyone should at least have an EHIC (European Health Insurance Card). This is supposed to provide free medical treatment with member states of the EU but the cover varies from state to state. You may wish to back up the EHIC with private medical insurance. Sailing outside the EU a good, comprehensive private medical insurance policy for each crew member is essential.

INSURANCE
Insurance companies are wary of single and short-handed sailors and frequently impose restrictions on passage length by insisting that single-handers are either in harbour or anchored during the hours of darkness. On longer passages they are likely to insist that a minimum number of qualified crew are on board. Even when such requirements are met they may also ask for higher premiums or increase the deductible (excess). Before sailing single- or short-handed read your policy carefully and, if necessary, speak to your insurance company before leaving. They might be reluctant to offer you comprehensive cover offshore but they may be happy offering third party cover while you are offshore and revert to comprehensive in coastal waters.

MANAGING THE PASSAGE PLAN
When Kaiser Wilhelm asked Field Marshal von Moltke if his plan to defeat the Allies would succeed, von Moltke answered, 'No plan survives contact with the enemy.' This is true of every passage plan. Even before you leave harbour, circumstances conspire to mock your foresight.

Successfully managing the passage plan requires you to constantly review and modify it in the light of reality. Or, to put it another way, continuously review past and present events and attempt to anticipate how they will affect your future actions. You must also decide if any change you want to make to Plan A can be achieved with onboard resources. If not, then you must think again. This is when all the information you collected before sailing becomes really valuable. It allows you to think broadband.

You can only review your plan if you know what it is. Write it down. Use a notebook or a series of cards, one for each topic. I scribble mine on paper, put them in clear plastic folders and leave them hanging on a clip board by the chart table. Whatever system you adopt it must keep the information in order, and if you scribble like me make sure that you can always read your own writing. In case you need to refer to pilots or tide tables mark the relevant pages with paper clips so that you can find them quickly with cold hands.

It is impossible to anticipate how events will differ from your plan but they will. It may be something as simple, and as common, as the weather forecast not matching actual weather. Changes to your plan may develop slowly and their full effects not become apparent for many hours or even days. Or they may arrive with appalling suddenness demanding an instant response. They may be almost invisible or brash and obvious. Whatever form they take they will only be dealt with by continually reviewing your plan.

What if you need to change course to avoid a nasty weather system or take advantage of a coming wind shift? Headwinds mean tacking along the mean line of advance but how long should each board be? Calms mean motoring, but how much fuel can you afford to use and will it make much difference in the end? Do you need to abandon your preferred route and adopt one of the alternatives? Modifications to your plan should come after thought, not as an afterthought or knee-jerk reaction.

'What if…?' thinking occupies a good part of the short-handed sailor's waking hours. What if that cloud brings a squall? What if I don't pick up Start Point light in the next half hour? What if I arrive off that drying harbour early (or late)? 'What if…?' can be micro-management by asking 'What shall I do if that ship over there changes course?' to macro management looking at weather patterns and asking where you want to be in several days' time to avoid bad weather.

'What if…?' thinking means that when the unexpected happens you have already calculated the effect of various options. It is unlikely any single option will provide a complete answer but taken together they represent a huge body of information fresh in your mind, which allows you to quickly discard unsuitable responses and arrive at a sensible and workable solution.

Perfect answers come with hindsight. In the real world solutions range from the absolutely wonderful but impracticable to the completely stupid and impossible. Somewhere in the middle are the grey answers; none is perfect but any one of several will work. It is far better to pick one of these (use a pin if you must) and execute it with all the enthusiasm and resources at your disposal, than to do nothing while you search for the perfect response. A successful grey solution will never produce results as good as the perfect answer, but well executed it will always produce better results than perfection not implemented at all.

10 Sleep Management

I do not like hardship. I sail for enjoyment and prefer the easy life. Being exhausted for days on end makes a fine story but not a good time. Some skippers sail with an informal watch system which more or less leaves the crew to decide for themselves who stands watch and when. Democracy may work for the occasional, short voyage but it can go very wrong. Time off watch is an important component of an enjoyable cruise.

Unless the short-handed skipper has worked out a watch-keeping system that strikes a balance between work and play, rest can be a pearl beyond price and every voyage a triumph of endurance over exhaustion. When I began single-handed sailing my thinking on fatigue management was a mixture of old wives' tales, urban myth and downright ignorance.

One of my best misapprehensions was that any reasonably fit person should be able to miss one night's sleep. Of course, there will be times they feel very tired but a cup of coffee will deal with those occasions. In the real world, they will become progressively less alert, and towards the end of the 24 hours it becomes easier to defer action than to take it. Staying on watch for 24 hours is possible, but it is not clever. Another common myth is that during a life or death crisis individuals can survive two or even three days without sleep. This may have a grain of truth but it means living on adrenaline and drawing on deep reserves of physical and nervous energy. Once the emergency is over and the imperative to stay awake is removed you collapse. Twelve hours rest, including eight hours sleep, are needed after staying awake for between 36 to 48 hours. Two or three days rest, including eight hours sleep each day, are needed to recover from three or four days of more or less continuous activity. This is not a basis for a regular watch system.

Nor are stimulants. Taking stimulants to remain awake appears superficially attractive, particularly in an emergency, but it is not recommended. Stimulants affect both mood and judgement. They work for only one or two days at most, after which you are finished for at least another couple of days. Caffeine is a stimulant and its consumption should be carefully controlled. There is some evidence that reducing caffeine intake re-sensitises you to its stimulant effects, so cutting caffeine consumption by at least half in the two or three days before casting off makes good sense. When at sea keep caffeine in the form of coffee or cola drinks or tea for the times you have to work through a trough in your circadian cycle. Remember, caffeine takes about 30 minutes to kick in and its effects last for three to four hours. Do not drink coffee ahead of a sleep period.

Time	Body Temperature
0000	37
0200	35.9
0400	35.7
0600	35.9
0800	36.4
1000	36.6
1200	37
1400	36.5
1600	37
1800	37.6
2000	38.2
2200	37.5
0000	37

Some single-handed sailors reckon that it is safer to sleep during daylight and organize their routine so that they work nights. This relies on believing that other vessels are far more likely to see you in daylight than at night. Since commercial vessels keep only a token visual lookout I suspect the odds on them sighting a yacht are about the same day or night and probably no higher than zero. It also assumes that you can reverse your circadian rhythm. You cannot. Your body clock is deep within your genes. Night shift watch-keepers are not as alert or productive as daytime watch-keepers because we are not programmed to work at night.

Anyway, under this system, unless you have fairly lengthy periods of sleep during the day before staying awake during the night the problem of having enough of the right kind of sleep is not solved.

Other single-handers believe that they can train themselves to survive on less than their normal ration of sleep. While people differ in the amount of sleep they take each night, and this varies with age and physical fitness, if you consistently have less sleep than you normally need then you will become tired. The bad news for the older sailor is that although you may sleep less, you are more quickly affected by lack of sleep and take longer to recover from long periods of wake-fulness. Sleep stages 3 and 4, which are essential for physical restoration, tend to be shorter in older people. The good news is that you perform best in the morning.

The notion that fatigue is a state of mind that you rise above by the application of willpower, self-discipline or motivation is a gung-ho fable. Nobody beats the clock. Fatigue is a physical condition brought on by a combination of total sleep loss, continuous hours of wakefulness (not necessarily the same as your total sleep loss), physical effort, environmental conditions and circadian time of day. When these factors attack together then you become very tired, very quickly and the chances of making a mistake, misjudgement or poor decision are unacceptably high. In laboratory experiments around a quarter of subjects display worrying falls in their performance after one day awake; no one has stayed awake for two days without displaying some drop in their performance. After two and a half days without sleep the performance of even the toughest, fittest and most resolute of subjects is seriously degraded.

I knew no better when I made my first long single-handed passage but the gods smiled and decided to overlook what turned out to be a display of baseless self-confidence. I was sailing from Gosport to Cherbourg, a trip I had made many times with a full crew. I reckoned that it would take about fourteen hours and, although on my crewed passages everyone stood their watch, having a solo watch-keeping system never occurred to me. I knew that I would be crossing busy shipping lanes and expected to spend most of the time in the cockpit.

I saw no problem in being up and about for the entire trip. Sometimes, my normal working day was longer than fourteen hours and I managed to stay awake without any special effort. I was about to learn that when you sail short-handed then on all but the shortest of passages some form of watch-keeping system is essential.

Problems sneaked up and stabbed me in the back. First, even though I had discussed the weather with the forecaster in the Southampton Met Office, there was, contrary to expectations, an unexpected lack of wind. Second, I was short of fuel because I had forgotten to fill the tank. Lastly, I made the mistake of starting off in the evening after a day's work. I had been up for nine or ten hours before I sailed. The tide pushed me to and fro as I dribbled across the Channel in great arcs and it was thirty hours before I finally reached Cherbourg. I had been awake through two nights and on my feet for over forty hours. It had been a tiring learning curve.

CAT NAPPING

After my Cherbourg trip I sailed, like many single-handers, on the kitchen timer. The aim is to cat nap for no longer than you think it will take another vessel to come over the horizon and claim right of way over the patch of water you presently occupy. The maths behind calculating how long you can cat nap are exactly the same as those for working out when you will pick up a light. You determine the distance to your horizon. Next, you make your best guess as to the average height above sea level of the bridge of the average commercial vessel and calculate the distance to their horizon. Add the two distances together and that is how far away you ought to sight another vessel.

Assume you are on a collision course. Add your boat speed and the other vessel's estimated speed together and calculate how long it will take you to meet. Deduct five minutes for safety's sake and that is the time you set on your kitchen timer.

Everybody uses different figures when working out their sums. Everyone swears theirs is the only correct answer but, regardless of what figure they arrive at, the greatest value of this system is that it gives you the confidence to nap at times of your choosing rather than staying on your feet until you collapse.

Cat napping has achieved intellectual respectability as 'power napping' or 'strategic napping'. A joint NASA/FAA study of aircrew on long haul flights found that when allowed to nap in the cockpit pilots fell asleep in just over five minutes and slept for about 25 minutes. The results showed that they maintained a consistently good level of performance throughout the flight and well above pilots who did not nap. The danger is allowing your naps to extend from light sleep into deep sleep, say napping for over thirty minutes. This is when you suffer sleep inertia. Sleep inertia describes the situation when you wake up and wonder what planet you are on. It can last for fifteen or twenty minutes and during that time you are operating well below par.

Use this technique with care. In 1984 the skipper of the yacht *Granholm* on a single-handed qualifying cruise, set the timer for 30 minutes, went below and was run down by the overtaking *TFL Express* whose watch officer was plotting their position and whose lookout was making a cup of tea.

It is not wise to cat nap as you approach a hazard such as a reef or overfalls. It is not a good idea in poor visibility when you should be in the cockpit all the time, and you must be on watch in traffic-separation systems and busy waters. Busy waters obviously include port approaches and, less obviously, the approaches to landfalls and choke points.

GPS has encouraged everyone to select more or less the same coordinates for landfall and then steer straight towards them. Sailing from Spain or Portugal everyone picks the south-west corner off the island of Porto Santo for their landfall in the Maderas. After several empty days boats begin popping up all over the horizon and all aiming to be first at your waypoint.

Choke points are where vessels naturally come together to round a headland, join traffic separation systems or enter a channel. In thick fog off Start Point a freighter came up on the VHF giving the position, course and speed of a yacht six miles off its bow. The figures agreed with my GPS. I was about to speak to the freighter and discuss a course of action when two other yachts that I could not see radioed that the message was for them!

Some sailors claim to exist for weeks on nothing but catnaps, often as short as ten minutes. I do not doubt their claims; I just question that ordinary mortals can follow their example. In a lumpy sea three days out from Falmouth I set the kitchen timer and curled up for my nap. I woke up six hours later. It took several moments to work this out and then, terrified out of my wits, I rushed to the cockpit. I had never left Mintaka sailing unattended for so long and in all the years I had relied on the kitchen timer I had never slept through its ring. There was nothing in sight; the wind and seas were about the same as when I went to sleep and Mintaka was cheerfully crashing towards La Coruña. Cat napping is not a substitute for proper sleep. It merely extends the length of time you stay awake and operational, or if you prefer, delays the moment when your body says, 'You are going to sleep.' And you do.

DEVISING A SLEEP-MANAGEMENT STRATEGY

This episode encouraged me to look closer into sleep-management. Without a sensible sleep-management strategy hopes for crossing the Atlantic were pie in the sky. There had to be some workable system but the tales of single-handed sailing were silent on this subject. As far as I could discover my heroes slept when they could and cat napped otherwise. Sleep-management literature was, ironically, largely concerned with promising insomniacs a good night's slumber.

I did discover that before I could develop a sleep management strategy I had to

- learn how to recognize fatigue ;
- know the causes of fatigue;
- understand the effects of fatigue;
- know the principles of the Circadian Rhythm;
- be able to apply the ideas behind the sleep cycle.

SIGNS OF FATIGUE

Every skipper should know the early indicators of fatigue and watch out for them in themselves and their crew. The huge overlap between the symptoms of fatigue and hypothermia does not matter. You could be suffering to some degree from both and the treatment for both is immediate warmth and rest.

From bitter experience I know it is extremely difficult to see in yourself what is obvious in others. You are aware that you are tired but you are sure that you will

SLEEP DISTRIBUTION in a NORMAL POPULATION	
Hours of Sleep	**%age Population**
3 – 4	8%
5 -6	15%
6 – 8	62%
8 - 10	13%
>11	2%

Note:
This shows that most people should be aiming for 6-8 hours of sleep a day. Older folk may only need 5-6 hours of sleep a day by very few folk can manage with less. Do not assume that you are one of them.

push through the fatigue and wake up in a moment or two.

The behavioural signs you display are easily ignored or explained away and the cognitive symptoms are missed because you are not thinking straight.

Micro sleeps, where you doze for around 30 seconds, are particularly dangerous. They are unavoidable when you are extremely tired, and are a major cause of poor performance. They contribute to a skewed view of the world. You may miss some part of a developing situation when asleep for a few seconds and fill the gaps using your imagination. If not roused from a micro sleep you can fall properly asleep. The only sure cure for micro sleeps is a decent sleep.

It is a vicious circle. You are not clever enough to see that you are tired and too stupid to take a rest. For the solo sailor perhaps the most reliable warning signs are the physical symptoms and when you recognize that you are displaying them then take a break, instantly, for you are well down the road to complete exhaustion.

CIRCADIAN RHYTHM

TIME	STATE
0700 – 1300	Once through sleep inertia you are heading for a peak. Between 0900-1000 hours short-term memory and logical reasoning are at their best. Concentration is at its best between 1100-1200 hours. Morning is a good time for daily checks: most people are at their most efficient during this period.
1300 – 1600	Minor trough or lull otherwise known as siesta time. A good time for a sleep cycle after a light lunch.
1600 – 2200	Peak between 1700-1800 hours body is at its physical peak: good time for physical tasks. Athletes often turn in their best performances in early evening events. Digestive system peaks around 1900-2000 hours.
2200 – 0700	Trough which reaches its nadir in the small hours of the morning: people are at their least efficient. The body is at its lowest ebb between 0300-0400 hours. Many accidents happen when folk work through this period. No regular tasks should be scheduled during this period.

Note Times vary with individuals

CAUSES OF FATIGUE

It goes without saying that the greatest contributor to fatigue is lack of sleep but other factors have substantial walk on roles. Poor-quality rest and sleep is almost as bad as none. If you rely solely on cat naps or do not keep yourself warm and dry when resting, even if sitting in the cockpit, or if your rest periods are continually interrupted, then you will become tired earlier, for longer.

If you work hard for long hours then, surprise, surprise, you become tired. Try to schedule regular heavy work so that it is spread throughout the day with time to recover between sessions.

If you experience poor visibility or heavy weather, or some defect or problem with the boat, you will be emotionally and physically stressed. If you or your crew have personal problems, even if they have been left ashore, then you will be stressed, and when you are stressed fatigue builds up more quickly than normal. Stress, along with environmental factors (noise, motion, cold and wet) and worry are common causes of insomnia. This is the ultimate irony; you are tired, want to sleep but cannot. Eating sensibly and regularly delays the onset of fatigue. Sugary foods and sweets boost blood sugar levels very quickly and give a burst of energy, but high blood-sugar levels are quickly followed by a near vertical fall and low blood sugar increases fatigue. Meals mainly of carbohydrates are thought to encourage sleep and those mostly of protein, wakefulness. Proteins are best digested in the morning and are good for breakfast. Eating a large meal just before going to sleep puts your digestive system into overdrive and prevents you sleeping. Mealtimes should not clash with sleep periods.

The most commonly available and used medicine on board yachts is the ubiquitous seasick pill. Some cause drowsiness and some very nearly qualify as sleeping tablets. It pays to be aware of who is taking them and monitor the effect.

CAUSES OF FATIGUE

SERIAL	SYMPTOM	REMARKS
1	Lack of sleep	Monitor your total sleep debt including the day or so before departure.
2	Broken sleep	Too much cat napping without any proper sleep has a limited half life.
3	Adverse environmental conditions	Be careful about staying too long in wet, cold cockpits. If working on deck, then when finished get into the cabin and have a warm drink.
4	Monotonous watch keeping or other activities	Sitting in the cockpit for the sake of it is not a good idea.
5	Poor or inadequate diet	Try to eat proper meals regularly.
6	Poor or inadequate fluid intake	If making a warm drink is too much effort than drink pop or fruit juice.
7	Strenuous physical work	After a bout of hard work take a rest.
8	Prolonged but not necessarily strenuous physical work	Long hours of not too strenuous work are just as tiring as a short bout of very strenuous work.
9	Heavy mental workload	Thinking is tiring.
10	Emotional strain	You may be worried about the weather, a landfall or what's happening at home. The result is the same …you tire more easily.

EFFECT OF FATIGUE

One study (Reference 1) showed that after 18 hours awake the blood alcohol count (BAC) of those taking part was 0.05%. After a further six sleepless hours it had risen to a BAC of 0.1%. Someone with a BAC of 0.1% is seven times more likely to have accident that a person with a BAC of zero. It is salutary to think as you wriggle up the Needles Channel after an overnight Channel crossing, that the law would not let you behind the wheel of a car. In New Jersey, USA, a driver who causes a fatal accident after being awake for 24 hours can be convicted of vehicular homicide.

What makes the results of this experiment scary is that the subjects had no sleep debt before beginning the experiment and were not asked to carry out any physical activities during it. They were students, young, fit and keen to prove it.

Another piece of research (Reference 2) showed that 24 hours of sustained activity resulted in a 25% performance drop and higher mental functions such as the ability to evaluate problems or assess incoming information deteriorated before more obvious signs of fatigue such as yawning or micro-sleeps appeared. The message is

SIGNS OF FATIGUE or SLEEP LOSS

SYMPTOM	REMARKS
Behavioural	
Excited/emotive outbursts	Some people are naturally excited but this refers to abnormal or uncharacteristic outbursts.
Irritable/bad tempered	Some people are always irritable and bad tempered but this refers to abnormal or uncharacteristic outbursts.
Impulsive and intolerant behaviour	Fatigue is characterised by poor team working. People become moody, argumentative and irritable. They are also more likely to ignore safety precautions.
Cold	Body temperatures falls when tired.
Anxiety	Worries needlessly over situations where they have no control and cannot affect the outcome.
Depression	Has a 'glass half empty' view of the world. May suffer from psychosomatic aches and ills.
Apathy	Has a 'could not care less' attitude; unobservant; slow too respond to questions/instructions/requests.
Cognitive	
Lack of concentration and alertness	Unable to prioritise tasks. Unable to organise tasks if prioritised.
Poor judgement and decision making	Unable to correctly carry out simple arithmetic. Unable to correctly assess developing situations.
Poor short-term memory	Wandering disconnected thoughts. Becomes easily distracted and forgets to complete tasks. Unable to retain or recall information such as bearing taken or course to steer.
Poor situational awareness	Visually…poor at judging speed, time and distance. Slow to respond, physically or mentally.
Perceptual tunnelling	Tends to focus on a single task.
Physical	
Eyelids droop	Eye strain and blurred vision is common.
Increased blinking	
Unable to stop yawning	
Slurred, slow speech	
Poor hand-to-eye coordination	Often drops items.
Micro-sleeps of around 30 seconds	
Trouble holding head up	

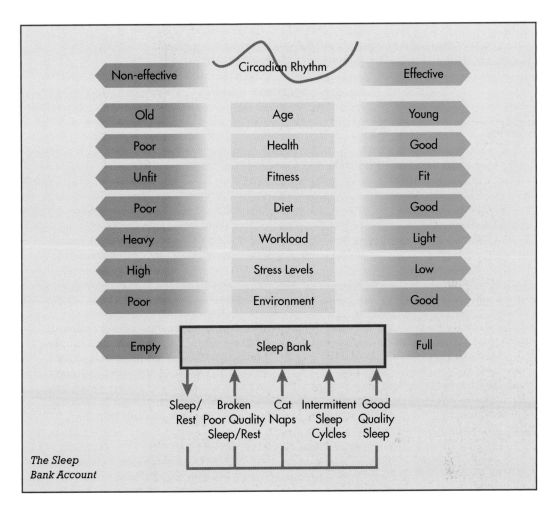

The Sleep Bank Account

clear; one day without sleep and you are drunk and incapable. After that it is all downhill.

CIRCADIAN RHYTHM

Some folk are night owls, meaning that they are lively and alert late at night and others are bright and smiling early in the morning, but this over simplifies a more complicated picture. Everyone has their own 24 hour body rhythm, called the circadian rhythm, where over 24 hours your level of alertness swings from peaks and troughs. Peaks are periods when you are at your sharpest and are good times for making decisions.

In the troughs you can be a hazard to everyone on board. Night-shift workers are almost twice as likely as day workers to have traffic accidents while travelling home from work. One common

strand to the accidents at the Three Mile Island nuclear power plant, Chernobyl nuclear disaster, and the Bophal chemical plant, and the decision to launch the Challenger space shuttle is that critical decisions were made in the small hours of the morning when those involved were at their least sharp.

THE SLEEP CYCLE

Sleep, even in solid blocks of eight hours, is made up of 90-minute cycles. Each cycle has five different stages. Cat napping takes you into the second stage of light sleep. Next comes deep sleep where you are dead to the world, then comes the rapid-eye-movement (REM) stage and finally you wake up. REM sleep is when you dream and experiments where volunteers are woken up the instant they reach this stage show that to remain

CAFFEINE CONTENT OF VARIOUS DRINKS and CHOCOLATE

DRINK	AMOUNT	CAFFEINE (mg)
Coffee	One cup	50 – 150
Tea	One cup	25 – 50
Cocoa	One cup	Less than 10
Milk Chocolate	50 gram bar	5 – 20
Dark Chocolate	50 gram bar	10 – 70
Cola-type drinks	One can	45 - 50

Notes
1. The caffeine content of coffee and tea varies depending on how much is used and the method of preparation. Decaffeinated coffee contains about as much caffeine as a cup of cocoa.
2. Diet cola-type drinks contain as much caffeine as non-diet colas.

healthy mentally we need our dreams. People deprived of REM sleep display signs of mental disturbance within days. REM sleep deficiency is characterised by irritability, disorientation and poor attention span. Extreme REM deficit can induce hallucinations. Single-handed sailors and others, Slocum and Shackleton included, have reported believing they were at times accompanied by helpful crew. Surviving solely on cat naps means we have no dreams, and instead meet up with the imaginary friends of our childhood.

Curiously the light sleep stage is by far the longest, occupying about half of each cycle and twice as much time as the deep sleep part of the cycle, which helps to explain why changes in wind strength, sea conditions, course and other external stimuli rouse you from your nap and not, as you may like to believe, your sixth sense or overworked guardian angel.

Once asleep, each phase slides into the next. The catch is falling asleep in the first place. This is not easy when your mind is churning problems over and over. Develop pre-sleep rituals to slow you down mentally and physically and prepare your body for sleep. These include reading a book for a few minutes, listening to a tape (through headphones if there are others onboard), drinking a cup of cocoa, perhaps simple meditation to clear the mind of the day's woes. If all else fails, try breathing deep and slow and counting sheep. When you wake up take a few moments to become fully awake before starting work.

COMBATING FATIGUE
The best way to fight fatigue is to take ample, regular, good quality sleep. On inshore passages of no more than 30 or 40 hours it is possible to survive on stages 1 and 2 of the sleep cycle for there is the promise of a good night's sleep when you reach harbour, before sleep debt and lack of proper sleep become a problem.

Monitor yourself and your crew for signs of fatigue. Keep a close watch for mental deterioration. Are you taking longer and longer to carry out the simple mental arithmetic, speed, time distance problems for example, of navigation? Are you quickly forgetting information such as the times of high water or the details of the latest weather forecast? A simple check for mental alertness is to pick a number between five and ten and then keep adding seven to it for one minute. If you do not succeed or begin stumbling over the figures then watch out for you are not as sharp as you thought.

STAGES IN THE SLEEP CYCLE

SLEEP STAGE	STATE	DURATION	TIME
Stage 1	transition state between wakefulness and sleep.	about 2-5 per cent of total sleep time.	2-6 minutes.
Stage 2	light sleep.	50 per cent of total sleep time.	45-55 minutes.
Stages 3 and 4	also called Slow Wave Sleep There is evidence that Stage 3 and 4 sleep, the most common in the first few hours of sleep, serves the function of physical and mental restoration. The amount of Stage 3 and 4 sleep increases after strenuous physical activity. Disturbances, such as a loud noises, interrupt the deeper sleep stages and take the sleeper back to lighter sleep stages.	about 20-25 per cent of total sleep time.	18-28 minutes.
Stage 5	Rapid Eye Movement (REM) sleep, where dreaming occurs.	about 20-25 per cent of total sleep time.	18-28 minutes.

A typical sleep cycle lasts around 90 to 110 minutes. Further cycles then occur until waking. It becomes progressively harder to rouse people as they pass deeper into the sleep cycle.

On longer passages organise routines so that everyone on board has several complete sleep cycles every day. A full night's sleep is made up of four or five cycles. The good news is you gain more or less the same benefits by taking your sleep in four or five separate cycles during the day. If you can, then the best time is in the troughs of your circadian rhythm when your body is ready for sleep.

This is when the effort to provide good sea berths for all aboard pays off. Bunking on a heap of wet sails makes for a good tale but not adequate rest. Ideally, sleeping cabins should be completely separate from work and social areas and provide quiet, dark sleeping quarters. Often this is out of the question but, as far as possible, sea bunks and their occupants should be isolated from the effects of the ship's normal routine. Anyone working below decks should make every effort to avoid disturbing those asleep. After all, it will be their turn off watch next.

11 Watch-keeping

When you have developed a sleep-management strategy then you are ready to put together a watch-keeping system. Whatever watch system you adopt you must enforce it from the moment you cast off. There is nothing worse than leaving harbour with everyone in the cockpit playing sailors and admiring the view as land falls astern. Four hours later a tired and cold off-duty watch suddenly discover that goofing in the cockpit is not watch-keeping and they have hours of work ahead of them.

WATCH-KEEPING SYSTEMS

Mariners once began each new day at local noon with the taking of a noon sight for latitude but, somewhat confusingly, the first watch of the traditional watch-keeping system began at 8.00 pm. Whenever you decide that a new day dawns is strictly between you and the log book.

On a long voyage the demands of sailing a boat short-handed can blur one day into the next. Instead of following the clock it is much wiser to base the daily routine round the principle of circadian rhythm. Duties should be arranged so that everyone has at least two or three unbroken sleep cycles per day and that regular tasks are not timetabled during troughs in the circadian rhythm. Yachts travel so slowly that jet lag is not a problem, though differing time zones means such items as weather forecasts and radio nets rarely fit neatly into your schedule, which must be adjusted to suit.

Whatever your preferred watch-keeping system have an alternative to hand that can be adopted if one or more of your crew cannot stand their watch. Ultimately, if you are the last man standing there is no choice. You must begin watch-keeping for one.

WATCH-KEEPING FOR ONE

If there is any single factor which distinguishes the single-handed sailor from the skipper with a crew it is the effort they devote to fatigue management. However poor the watch-keeping system on a fully crewed boat most onboard

---

WATCH-KEEPING FOR ONE

TIME	CIRCADIAN STATE	Action solo
0700 – 1300	Peak: good time for daily checks: people are at their most efficient.	Breakfast Personal admin Daily checks Navigation Lunch
1300 – 1600	Minor trough or lull otherwise known as siesta time.	Sleep/rest
1600 – 2200	Peak another good time for regularly scheduled tasks.	Ship's housekeeping Maintenance Dinner
2200 – 0700	Trough which reaches its nadir in the small hours of the morning: People are at their least efficient. No regular tasks should be scheduled during this period.	Sleep/rest

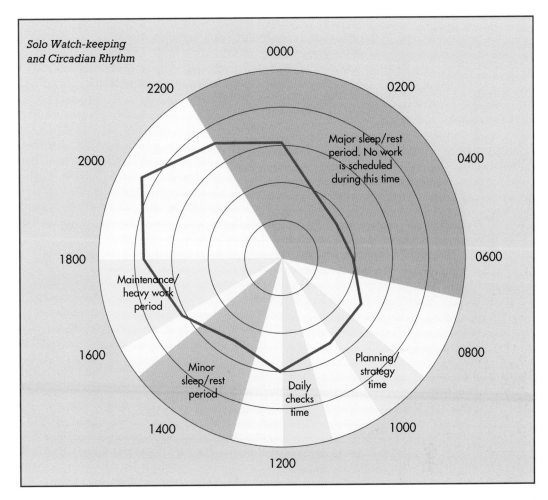

Solo Watch-keeping and Circadian Rhythm

0000
0200
0400
0600
0800
1000
1200
1400
1600
1800
2000
2200

Major sleep/rest period. No work is scheduled during this time

Maintenance/ heavy work period

Minor sleep/rest period

Daily checks time

Planning/ strategy time

can count on some rest some of the time, but unless the single-handed skipper is very careful there is no rest for him at any time.

He has no choice of watch-keeping systems. He is on watch all day, every day, and must be prepared to work the boat any hour of the day or the night. There is no perfect solution to how he obtains sufficient rest but find it he must. Every voyage is begun with a finite reserve of energy and no matter how miserly it is hoarded, however carefully it is spent, irreplaceable capital is slowly eroded. Success is managing this energy reserve so as to arrive safely at your destination before being declared bankrupt.

It is important to start every voyage free of sleep debt. This rules out the all-night leaving party the day before and, once at sea, he should organize his day around his circadian rhythm with the aim of taking sleep in complete cycles during the troughs if possible and cat napping at every opportunity. Whenever possible, decision making, navigation and other regular tasks are scheduled to be carried out during peaks in his circadian cycle. This breaks his day into a series of phases when specific types of tasks are carried out and this, in turn, imposes a structure and discipline to the day. It is one thing to identify some maintenance, and schedule it to be done in the maintenance period later that day. It is quite another to postpone it to sometime, never.

SEA ROUTINES
The real world may not always fit in round your circadian rhythm. Single-handers must

SEA ROUTINES on a TYPICAL PASSAGE

CASTING OFF OR DEPARTURE ROUTINE	From: pontoon or leaving anchorage until in channel or open water: From: leaving harbour and sailing to channel or open water. Duration: probably no more than 30 minutes. Navigation: by eye. Action: crew stow warps, fenders, anchors.
BUSY WATERS ROUTINE	From: leaving harbour and sailing to point of departure. Duration: unlikely to exceed five or six hours. Navigation: by pilotage. Action: once stowed for sea crew stand their watches.
SHORT PASSAGE ROUTINE	From: leaving the point of departure until clear of traffic separation systems and off-soundings. Duration: probably covers the first 40 hours of a passage and includes coastal and cross-channel passages. Navigation: by GPS or DR whichever you prefer. Action: crew stand their watches. If you have three in your crew you may wish to adopt a watch-keeping system with two on watch at any one time: If single-handed, rest is taken in cat naps whenever and as often as circumstances allow.
LONG PASSAGE ROUTINE	From: clearing traffic separation lanes and going off soundings to entering TSS or coming onto soundings. Duration: this routine can last for several weeks. Navigation: by GPS, DR, astro whichever you prefer. Action: crew stand their watches. If you have three in your crew you may wish to adopt a watch-keeping system with only one person on watch at any time: if solo watch taking sleep in complete cycles as circumstances permits.
SHORT PASSAGE ROUTINE	From: re-entering soundings to point of arrival. Duration: probably covers the last 40 hours of a passage. Navigation: by GPS or DR whichever you prefer. Action: crew stand their watches. If you have three in your crew you may wish to revert to a watch-keeping system with two on watch at any time: if single-handed rest is taken in cat naps whenever and as often circumstances allow.
BUSY WATERS ROUTINE	From: Point of arrival to harbour or anchorage. Duration: unlikely to exceed five or six hours. Navigation: by pilotage. Action: duty watch tidies ship: if going foreign hoist courtesy ensign and check ship's and crews' papers: ready warps, fenders, anchors.
BERTHING OR ANCHOR ROUTINE	From: entering harbour to berth or anchorage. Duration: probably no more than 30 minutes. Navigation: by eye. Action: watch-keeping abandoned: crew prepare warps, fenders, anchors. Berth or anchor ship.

PLYMOUTH TO BREST

Passage Routines, Estimated Speed Made Good is 5 knots, Estimated Time En Route is 36 hours

TIME	ACTION	PASSAGE ROUTINE
04 JULY		
0600	Depart Millbay Marina	Harbour Routine
0645	Abeam Penlee Point	Busy Water Routine
0700		Busy Water Routine
0800		Busy Water Routine
0830	Off Eddystone	Busy Water Routine
0900		Short Passage Routine
1000		Short Passage Routine
1100		Short Passage Routine
1200		Short Passage Routine
1300		Short Passage Routine
1400		Short Passage Routine
1500		Short Passage Routine
1600		Short Passage Routine
1700		Short Passage Routine
1800		Short Passage Routine
1900	Approaching Ushant TSS	Busy Water Routine
2000		Busy Water Routine
2100		Busy Water Routine
2200		Busy Water Routine
2300		Busy Water Routine
2400		Busy Water Routine
05 JULY		Busy Water Routine
0100		Busy Water Routine
0200		Busy Water Routine
0300		Busy Water Routine
0400		Busy Water Routine
0445	Ushant TSS	Busy Water Routine
0500		Busy Water Routine
0600		Busy Water Routine
0700		Busy Water Routine
0715	Ushant	Busy Water Routine
0800		Busy Water Routine
0900		Busy Water Routine
1000		Busy Water Routine
1045	Landfall	Busy Water Routine
1100		Busy Water Routine
1200		Busy Water Routine
1300		Busy Water Routine
1400		Busy Water Routine
1415	POA	Harbour Routine
1500		Harbour Routine
1600	Arrive Moulin Blanc Marina	Harbour Routine

RED = CIRCADIAN TROUGH. LIGHT GREY = CIVIL TWILIGHT. GREEN = CIRCADIAN PEAK
DARK GREY = NAUTICAL TWILIGHT. BLACK = NIGHT

vary their watch-keeping system to suit circumstances of the moment and still find opportunities for rest. In coastal and offshore waters with their traffic-separation systems and objective dangers, it is stupid and dangerous to sleep for ninety minutes at a stretch. In some waters even napping for twenty minutes is not feasible. Adopting one particular watch-keeping system and sticking to it regardless or abandoning it and snatching sleep between off the cuff responses to events will not work. You must be in control. One option is to have a range of sea routines reflecting the demands made at different points in any passage.

Consider sailing between Plymouth to Brest. A night at sea is unavoidable and your departure time will be determined by the need for a fair tide round Ushant.

Busy-Water Routine

Having cleared the marina and found a quiet patch of water to stow warps and fenders you wriggle past Drake Island towards Penlee Point. In these very busy waters leaving the cockpit is impossible and you will probably be helming. Forget rest. Dashing into the cabin for a pilot or chart is out of the question. Have all the information you MAY need to hand in the cockpit. I think of this as my harbour routine and if entering or leaving harbour at night or poor visibility I would also have a torch or a foghorn in the cockpit.

Short-Passage Routine

Off Penlee Point the self-steering is engaged. Freed from the tyranny of the tiller you lay a course to leave Eddystone Light safely to port. Life is more relaxed but it is probably unwise to leave the cockpit for more than a minute or two until Eddystone and the shipping off the English coast is well astern. Now can wind up the egg timer and begin napping for as often as circumstances allow. Once well offshore it may just be possible to put in one or two complete 90-minute sleep cycles during the afternoon circadian trough to prepare you for the night ahead. Whether this is possible depends on wind and sea conditions, visibility, other traffic and whether or not you have a radar detector aboard.

Around sunset you will be approaching the traffic separation zones off Ushant. These can be very busy waters and there are two schools of thought about crossing shipping lanes at night. The first believes that it is easier to spot other shipping and determine their course and aspect by their lights, and the other does not. Whichever viewpoint you support it is best to have the engine running and aim to slip under the sterns of commercial ships rather than cut in front of their bows. It may prove necessary from time to time to disengage the self-steering, slow down or even hove-to to let other vessels sail clear. Almost all the time in the shipping lanes will be spent in the cockpit following your busy-water routine until you are round Ushant and you are able to return to your short-passage routine. Once you make your landfall you return to your busy-water routine and then as you make you way to the marina.

On a longer passage, say, from Falmouth to La Coruña in north-west Spain. You would follow a very similar watch-keeping pattern until you cleared Ushant. Ushant would be given a much wider berth and shortly afterwards you sail off soundings and into tolerably empty waters. You can now begin taking sleep in complete cycles. Most egg timers run for no more than an hour so you may have to set an alarm clock to be sure of waking up. This is your long-passage routine.

As you approach the Spanish coast you will begin meeting more traffic and move back into your short-passage routine until you make your landfall, and adopt your busy-water routine until you reach your berth.

Passage routines allow you to choose when to switch from one to another. You are in charge. You know why you have adopted a particular routine and how long you expect it to last: although this may be to the end of a specific event rather than a specified time. Some of these phases can be written into your passage plan so that you know, well ahead of time, when you are likely to spend long hours awake and, if circumstances permit, you can top up your sleep bank beforehand.

DAILY CHECKS

ITEM	DONE	REMARKS
Sea Cocks		
Heads		
Bilges		
Bilge Pumps		
Hatches and deck fittings		
General stowage		
Galley and ready to use supplies		
Long term stowage		
Standing rigging		
Running rigging		
Winches and cleats		
Sails		
Chafe check		
Electronic equipment		
Electrics		
Batteries		
Fuel, oil and lubricants		
Water		
Engine and machinery		
Safety equipment		
Windvane		
Electronic self-steering		

They are not timetables to be followed blindly. Rather they are a guide to helping you maximise your rest and at any stage in your passage the routine you adopt will be dictated by the circumstances you encounter and not the plan you wrote up before leaving harbour.

Anchor Watches

When you are tired on single- or short-handed coastal passages, creeping into a quiet cove or sheltered bay and dropping the hook is a good way of catching up on sleep. Whether you keep an anchor watch or not probably depends on weather conditions and how much faith you have in the anchor holding. It is a good idea to set the anchor alarm on the GPS to a range that just exceeds your turning circle as you swing with the tide or wind. Have a second anchor complete with anchor chain or line on the foredeck ready to go. Then if you do drag you receive early warning and if letting out more chain or line does not resolve the problem you have the choice of putting to sea or laying a second anchor. If the holding is poor or the weather unkind then it may be necessary to keep watch on the egg timer in order to monitor conditions. This is almost as tiring as being on passage.

When you are short-handed it is a good idea to put out an over generous amount of anchor chain or line in order to give the anchor the best possible chance of catching and keeping a hold.

SHIP'S HOUSEKEEPING

The ship's housekeeping is an important part of the short- and long-passage routines. These are the daily checks and any necessary maintenance to confirm all is well. It helps to keep a list of these tasks along with who is responsible for carrying out each task pinned up by the chart table. This is important, or willing horses are worked to death. Having a list shares the work out and if duties are logged on completion, the skipper can check if they have been carried out (and with what result) without having to nag the crew.

The single-hander has no doubt who is responsible for these checks but pin the list up by the chart table anyway and tick them off as you do them each day. If you notice a couple of days have gone by since the last checks were made then you are slipping and should take steps to pull your socks up.

AIDS TO WATCH-KEEPING

The yachtsman can call upon electronic aids to support the human eyeball in keeping a lookout. Many yachts have radar and although they may not have sufficient electrical power to drive the radar day and night most radars have a sleep mode where they carry out one or two sweeps every few minutes. If these sweeps detect a target, the radar sounds a warning to alert the crew and comes up to full power.

If you do not have radar then a radar detector like a CARD (Collison Avoidance Radar Detector) is a good second best. Every time the radar of another ship strikes yours the radar detector sounds an alarm and its beep, beep, beep is like a persistent alarm clock. It also gives some idea of the relative bearing of the other vessel and even if it is approaching or going away. Unfortunately in busy waters it simply tells you that you are surrounded. Off-soundings where ships come one at a time the CARD works extremely well and gives good advance warning of approaching shipping. Radar detectors draw only milliamps and can run all day every day.

Another option is to fit a radar target enhancer. This not only acts as a radar detector but when struck by another vessel's radar sends back a powerful active signal rather than the passive reflection from a radar reflector, and you appear as a bright, prominent blip on the other vessel's radar screen. Radar enhancers use much more power than a radar detector but less than a radar.

The Automatic Identification System (AIS) is coming on stream. The idea is that every ship within range appears, relative to yours, on a display along with its name, call sign and other information. The present thinking is that leisure craft carry a receiver and commercial vessels a transceiver so that the screen is not cluttered with too much information from too many ships. Safety with this system lies in every commercial vessel carrying an AIS transceiver, which makes it only slightly better than coming up on the VHF every 15-20 minutes with an all ships security broadcast giving your position, course and speed and asking vessels to keep a look out for you.

Electronic watch-keeping aids can provide the confidence to go off watch and rest knowing that if another vessel does sail over the horizon there will be ample warning of its approach.

They are especially valuable in poor visibility or at night.

WATCH-KEEPING FOR TWO

With two onboard and if your boat is set up for single-handed sailing, then watch and watch is a good system. I like working four-hour watches with dog watches so that the graveyard watch of midnight to four in the morning comes on alternate nights. You can count on a long nap during the day and a couple of sleep periods when you are off watch during the night.

The Swedish watch and watch system uses a mixture of four-, five- and six-hour watches to achieve the same effect as dog watches.

Four hours off watch does not equate to fours hours of sleep. Only fictional heroes make the transition from sound sleep to man of action instantly. When handing over a watch allow time not only for those coming on watch to dress and have a hot drink but also time for those going off watch to hand over properly and, if at night, for those coming on watch to acquire their full night vision. At least another ten or fifteen minutes is spent going to sleep and waking up. Add everything up and four hours off watch probably equates to between two and three hours sleep, if you are lucky. Some cruising couples prefer working four hours watches during the day and three hours at night. The usual argument advanced for this is that the demands of a three-hour watch in the depths of the night are about the same as a four-hour watch in the afternoon. I'm not sure if this is true but it does guarantee less than two hours' continuous sleep when you need it most. When both can take command then watch and watch systems work well. The Hiscocks sailed

SWEDISH WATCH SYSTEM			
Time	Hours on Watch	Day 1	Day 2
0000 - 0400	4	B	A
0400 - 0800	4	A	B
0800 – 1300	5	B	A
1300 -1900	6	A	B
1900 – 2400	5	B	A

WATCH-KEEPING FOR TWO

Time	A	B	Day 1	Day 2
0000 – 0400	Off watch and asleep.	On watch, lookout, sailing trimming and navigation. Prepares drinks for 0345 and wakes A.	B	A
0400 – 0800	On watch, lookout, sailing trimming and navigation. Prepares breakfast for 0745 and wakes B.	Off watch and asleep.	A	B
0800 – 1200	Off watch but assists with daily checks, navigation, rests, Personal admin.	On watch, carries out daily checks, navigation, personal admin. Prepares lunch for noon. Wakes A at 1145.	B	A
1200 – 1600	On watch. Cleans up after lunch. On watch, lookout, sailing trimming and navigation. Prepares drinks for 1745 and wakes B.	Off watch resting.	A	B
1600 – 1800	Off watch resting.	On watch. Prepares dinner wakes A at 1730.	B	A
1800 – 2000	On watch. Cleans up after dinner. Ship's housekeeping and maintenance checks. Makes drinks and wakes B at 1945.	Off watch but assists with ship's housekeeping and maintenance checks. Rests.	A	B
2000 – 2400	Off watch and asleep.	On watch, lookout, sailing trimming and navigation. Prepares drinks for 2345 and wakes A.	B	A

This is on a two-day cycle. The two dog watches, first dog 1600-1800 and last dog 1800-2000 means that each crew member stands the midnight to four o'clock watch on alternate nights.

round the world standing watch and watch, and on their first circumnavigation did not have a self-steering system. If only the skipper is capable of standing a watch then the other crew member is primarily a lookout and it will be rare for the skipper to have more than two hours' unbroken sleep.

CALLING THE SKIPPER

It is important that the crew know when their scope for decision making runs out and they must make the skipper aware of what is happening. If you are sailing with family or friends it may sound pompous or dictatorial to point out there is a chain of command with you at the top. A court will have no such reluctance when allocating blame. The instruction 'Call me if you need me' is too vague and not enough, especially if the crew is inexperienced. The circumstances in which the skipper wishes to be called should be written up in the logbook and end with the awful phrase…'and call me at any time when you are in the least doubt as to what is happening or what action to take.' The times you may wish to be called can include the approach of another vessel, receiving a gale warning, changes in wind strength or

WATCH-KEEPING FOR THREE

Time	A DAY 1	B DAY 1	C DAY 1	Day 2	Day 3
0000–0400	Off watch and asleep.	On watch, lookout, sailing trimming and navigation. Prepares drinks for 0345 and wakes A.	Off watch and asleep.	C	A
0400–0800	On watch, lookout, sailing trimming and navigation. Prepares breakfast for 0745 and wakes B+C.	Off watch and asleep.	Off watch and asleep.	B	B
0800–1200	Off watch.	Off watch.	On watch, carries out daily checks, personal admin, ship's housekeeping, navigation. Prepares lunch for noon. Wakes A at 1145.	A	C
1200–1600	Off watch.	On watch. Cleans up after lunch On watch, lookout, sailing trimming and navigation.	Off watch.	C	A
1600–1800	On watch. Prepares dinner wakes B+C at 1730.	Off watch.	Off watch.	B	B
1800–2000	Off watch.	Off watch.	On Watch. Cleans up after dinner, rests. Makes drinks and wakes B at 1945.	A	C
2000–2400	Off watch and asleep.	On watch, lookout, sailing trimming and navigation. Prepares drinks for 2345 and wakes A.	Off watch and asleep.	C	A

direction, picking up a light, decreasing visibility and alterations in course.

WATCH-KEEPING FOR THREE

From around the second half of the 16th century the ship's day was split into five, four one-hour watches and two, two hour dog watches. Crews were divided into port (larboard) and starboard watches. They stood watch and watch with the passage of time measured by a half-hour sandglass. The turning of the glass at the end of one half an hour and the beginning of the next was marked by striking the ship's

bell. In a four-hour watch there are eight bells. As part of a 19th-century reform package, Royal Navy crews were divided into three watches working four hours on, eight hours off and this was a major factor in improving sailors' overall health.

In every three-watch system one watch has the deck and sails the ship; one watch, the next on, is off duty but on standby; and the third watch is off duty. With any luck the standby watch will not be called. In this system, everyone has a politician's promise of at least six to seven

WATCH-KEEPING FOR THREE MOTHER-WATCH SYSTEM

Time	A DAY 1	B DAY 1	C DAY 1 C IS MOTHER	DAY 2 B IS MOTHER	DAY 3 A IS MOTHER
0000– 0400	Off watch and asleep.	On watch, lookout, sailing trimming and navigation. Prepares drinks for 0345 and wakes A.	Mother asleep.	A	C
0400– 0800	On watch, lookout, sailing trimming and navigation. Prepares drinks for 0745 and wakes B+C.	Off watch and asleep.	Mother asleep.	C	B
0800– 1200	Off watch but assists with daily checks, navigation, rests. Personal admin.	On watch, carries out daily checks, navigation. Personal admin.	Mother prepares breakfast. Personal admin, ship's house-keeping. Prepares lunch for noon and wakes A at 1145.	A	C
1200– 1600	On watch. Cleans up after lunch. On watch, lookout, sailing trimming and navigation.	Off watch resting.	Mother prepares drinks for 1745 and wakes B.	C	B
1600– 1800	Off watch resting.	On watch.	Mother prepares dinner wakes A at 1730.	A	C
1800– 2000	On watch. Maintenance checks. Makes drinks and wakes B at 1945.	Off watch but assists with maintenance checks. Rests.	Mother cleans up after dinner, rests.	C	B
2000– 2400	Off watch and asleep.	On watch, lookout, sailing trimming and navigation.	Mother rests. Prepares drinks for 2345 and wakes A.	A	C

hours' unbroken sleep a day, although it is not always taken during the night. Alternatively, you can run a mother-watch system where two of the crew stand watch and watch and the third member is mother, responsible for the ship's housekeeping and cooking. Everyone can then expect a full night's sleep every third night.

ROLLING-WATCH SYSTEM

This is for boats with three or more in the crew.

Instead of teams of watch-keepers you decide how many warm bodies constitute a watch and then every hour one is replaced by someone who is off watch. Proponents of this system claim it increases social interaction and there is less overcrowding below at change of watch. On the downside it is difficult to administer. It is easy to lose track of who is on or off watch, and the responsibly for carrying out daily checks including cooking and cleaning ship becomes

ROLLING WATCH SYSTEM

TIME	THREE ON BOARD		FOUR ON BOARD	
	ON WATCH	OFF WATCH	ON WATCH	OFF WATCH
KEEPING ONE-HOUR WATCHES				
0000 – 0100	A	B+C	A	B+C+D
0100 – 0200	B	A+C	B	A+C+D
0200 – 0300	C	A+B	C	A+B+D
0300 – 0400	A	B+C	D	A+B+C
0400 – 0500	B	A+C	A	B+C+D
0500 – 0600	C	A+B	B	A+C+D
0600 – 0700	A	B+C	C	A+B+D
0700 – 0800	B	A+C	D	A+B+C
0800 – 0900	C	A+B	A	B+C+D
0900 – 1000	A	B+C	B	A+C+D
1000 – 1100	B	A+C	C	A+B+D
1100 – 1200	C	A+B	D	A+B+C
1200 – 1300	A	B+C	A	B+C+D
1300 – 1400	B	A+C	B	A+C+D
1400 – 1500	C	A+B	C	A+B+D
1500 – 1600	A	B+C	D	A+B+C
1600 – 1700	B	A+C	A	B+C+D
1700 – 1800	C	A+B	B	A+C+D
1800 – 1900	A	B+C	C	A+B+D
1900 – 2000	B	A+C	D	A+B+C
2000 – 2100	C	A+B	A	B+C+D
2100 – 2200	A	B+C	B	A+C+D
2200 – 2300	B	A+C	C	A+B+D
2300 – 2400	C	A+B	D	A+B+C
KEEPING TWO-HOUR WATCHES				
0000 – 0200	A	B+C	A	B+C+D
0200 – 0400	B	A+C	B	A+C+D
0400 – 0600	C	A+C	C	A+B+D
0600 – 0800	A	B+C	D	A+B+C
0800 – 1000	B	A+C	A	B+C+D
1000 – 1200	C	A+C	B	A+C+D
1200 – 1400	A	B+C	C	A+B+D
1400 – 1600	B	A+C	D	A+B+C
1600 – 1800	C	A+C	A	B+C+D
1800 – 2000	A	B+C	B	A+C+D
2000 – 2200	B	A+C	C	A+B+D
2200 – 2400	C	A+C	D	A+B+C

confused. I have only sailed with this system twice, when its disadvantages dominated, and I did not like it. Rarely have I seen such a dispirited crew. However, with a willing and responsible crew it is worth considering.

With three, this system produces a rolling one hour on watch and two hours off. With four this becomes one hour on watch and three off. It may be wiser to extend the time on watch to two hours, which produces two hours on watch and four off. With a crew of four this will give everyone two on and six off.

DEMANDS OF NIGHT SAILING

Apart from knowing your lights the demands of night sailing are, in theory, not any different from day sailing, but yacht navigation lights are almost invisible to other vessels. Other yachts will see your lights but only when they are close. To commercial vessels with their policy of single manning and near-complete reliance on a radar watch, your lights do not exist.

Safety lies is assuming other vessels will not see you and that your radar return is lost in the clutter. On my Cherbourg trip I copied

Chichester and hung a Tilley lamp in the rigging to alert other to my presence, and discovered that I could see nothing beyond a narrow cone of light. This was scary. The modern equivalent is a strobe; fishing boats use them to mark nets and lines and sometimes themselves. The flashes blind you but if a watch officer does look out of his bridge windows then not only are strobes much brighter than a Tilley lamp but a flash is more obvious than a fixed light.

It is best to switch on a strobe only after seeing an approaching vessel and announcing your presence and intentions over the VHF. Traditionally, yachtsmen drew attention to their existence by either shining a torch on their sails or igniting a white flare. The less said about shining a light on the sails the better. It is a very poor second to shining the light directly at the other vessels and wiping it back and forth across their bridge. The lenses and reflectors in a torch are designed to push out a bright beam of light. A sail is not. The disadvantage of a flare is that it has a burn time of about 30 seconds and costs several pounds, unlike a strobe which costs about the same and lasts indefinitely.

RHYTHM OF PASSAGE MAKING

Every passage has it highs and lows. Heavy weather, changes of plan or illness can completely disrupt the ship's routine.

Sometimes you are so busy and so tired that you fail to notice that you are responding to events rather than controlling them. It is important to recognise when you have abandoned your routine and understand why, so that it can be re-established as soon as possible. Never skip the daily checks however reluctant you are to carry them out.

Highs and lows include your state of mind. Sometimes all is well and sailing is the most wonderful activity in the world. At others, and sometimes for no apparent reason, the world is grey and dark and growing blacker with every breath. Every so often the urge to be ashore is so strong that you would gladly trade your grandmother for a seat under a tree.

Between the Cape Verde Islands and Barbados I sailed a thousand miles non-stop for the first time. At happy hour that evening I celebrated this achievement. I went to sleep chuffed to bits and woke up next morning with my morale oozing out my boots, only too aware that I was only half way through my voyage, a thousand miles from anywhere and all alone on a very large ocean. I do not know what triggers these changes of mood. I do know nothing lasts forever and when spirits are down it is best to focus on the positive, plod on until the mood has passed until once again there is nothing so wonderful as messing about in boats.

TRADITIONAL WACTHES

BELLS	FIRST	MIDDLE	MORNING NOON	FORE NOON	AFTER DOG	FIRST DOG	LAST
8	2000	2400	0400	0800	1200	1600	1800
1	2030	0030	0430	0830	1230	1630	1830
2	2100	0100	0500	0900	1300	1700	1900
3	2130	0130	0530	0930	1330	1730	1930
4	2200	0200	0600	1000	1400		
5	2230	0230	0630	1030	1430		
6	2300	0300	0700	1100	1500		
7	2330	0330	0730	1130	1530		
8	2400	0400	0800	1200	1600	1800	2000

Note:
1. Sometimes the First Dog Watch is called Lookout and the Last Dog Watch becomes the Dog watch.
2. Anchor watches were called 'quarter watches' because only a quarter of the crew were on watch.

You rely on us.
Can we rely on you?

Become an Offshore member from just £5.00 per month.

Last year, our volunteers saved over 7,000 people. But we couldn't have saved a single one of them without the support of people like you. Join Offshore today, and you'll be helping to run the Lifeboat service whose volunteers will be on hand, should you ever get into difficulty at sea.

Call **0800 543210** today.

Or visit **www.rnli.org.uk**

Offshore

FOS2004

registered charity no. 209603